P9-BJL-680

Africa

Opposing Viewpoints ®

Laura K. Egendorf, *Book Editor*

Bruce Glassman, *Vice President*
Bonnie Szumski, *Publisher*
Helen Cothran, *Managing Editor*

OPPOSING
VIEWPOINTS®
SERIES

GREENHAVEN PRESS
An imprint of Thomson Gale, a part of The Thomson Corporation

THOMSON
™
GALE

Detroit • New York • San Francisco • San Diego • New Haven, Conn.
Waterville, Maine • London • Munich

LIBRARY OF CONGRESS CATALOGING-IN-PUBLICATION DATA

Africa / Laura K. Egendorf, book editor.
    p. cm. — (Opposing viewpoints series)
Includes bibliographical references and index.
ISBN 0-7377-2218-5 (lib. : alk. paper) — ISBN 0-7377-2219-3 (pbk. : alk. paper)
    1. Africa—Social policy. 2. Africa—Economic policy. 3. Africa—Politics and government—1960– . I. Egendorf, Laura K., 1973– . II. Series. III. Opposing viewpoints series (Unnumbered)
HN773.5.A3 2005
361.6'1'096—dc22   2004042432

Printed in the United States of America

AUGUSTANA LIBRARY
UNIVERSITY OF ALBERTA

"Congress shall make no law...abridging the freedom of speech, or of the press."

First Amendment to the U.S. Constitution

The basic foundation of our democracy is the First Amendment guarantee of freedom of expression. The Opposing Viewpoints Series is dedicated to the concept of this basic freedom and the idea that it is more important to practice it than to enshrine it.

Contents

Why Consider
Opposing Viewpoints?

"The only way in which a human being can make some approach to knowing the whole of a subject is by hearing what can be said about it by persons of every variety of opinion and studying all modes in which it can be looked at by every character of mind. No wise man ever acquired his wisdom in any mode but this."

John Stuart Mill

In our media-intensive culture it is not difficult to find differing opinions. Thousands of newspapers and magazines and dozens of radio and television talk shows resound with differing points of view. The difficulty lies in deciding which opinion to agree with and which "experts" seem the most credible. The more inundated we become with differing opinions and claims, the more essential it is to hone critical reading and thinking skills to evaluate these ideas. Opposing Viewpoints books address this problem directly by presenting stimulating debates that can be used to enhance and teach these skills. The varied opinions contained in each book examine many different aspects of a single issue. While examining these conveniently edited opposing views, readers can develop critical thinking skills such as the ability to compare and contrast authors' credibility, facts, argumentation styles, use of persuasive techniques, and other stylistic tools. In short, the Opposing Viewpoints Series is an ideal way to attain the higher-level thinking and reading skills so essential in a culture of diverse and contradictory opinions.

In addition to providing a tool for critical thinking, Opposing Viewpoints books challenge readers to question their own strongly held opinions and assumptions. Most people form their opinions on the basis of upbringing, peer pressure, and personal, cultural, or professional bias. By reading carefully balanced opposing views, readers must directly confront new ideas as well as the opinions of those with whom they disagree. This is not to simplistically argue that everyone who reads opposing views will—or should—change his or her opinion. Instead, the series enhances readers' understanding of their own views by encouraging confrontation with opposing ideas. Careful examination of others' views can lead to the readers' understanding of the logical inconsistencies in their own opinions, perspective on why they hold an opinion, and the consideration of the possibility that their opinion requires further evaluation.

Evaluating Other Opinions

To ensure that this type of examination occurs, Opposing Viewpoints books present all types of opinions. Prominent spokespeople on different sides of each issue as well as well-known professionals from many disciplines challenge the reader. An additional goal of the series is to provide a forum for other, less known, or even unpopular viewpoints. The opinion of an ordinary person who has had to make the decision to cut off life support from a terminally ill relative, for example, may be just as valuable and provide just as much insight as a medical ethicist's professional opinion. The editors have two additional purposes in including these less known views. One, the editors encourage readers to respect others' opinions—even when not enhanced by professional credibility. It is only by reading or listening to and objectively evaluating others' ideas that one can determine whether they are worthy of consideration. Two, the inclusion of such viewpoints encourages the important critical thinking skill of objectively evaluating an author's credentials and bias. This evaluation will illuminate an author's reasons for taking a particular stance on an issue and will aid in readers' evaluation of the author's ideas.

It is our hope that these books will give readers a deeper understanding of the issues debated and an appreciation of the complexity of even seemingly simple issues when good and honest people disagree. This awareness is particularly important in a democratic society such as ours in which people enter into public debate to determine the common good. Those with whom one disagrees should not be regarded as enemies but rather as people whose views deserve careful examination and may shed light on one's own.

Thomas Jefferson once said that "difference of opinion leads to inquiry, and inquiry to truth." Jefferson, a broadly educated man, argued that "if a nation expects to be ignorant and free . . . it expects what never was and never will be." As individuals and as a nation, it is imperative that we consider the opinions of others and examine them with skill and discernment. The Opposing Viewpoints Series is intended to help readers achieve this goal.

David L. Bender and Bruno Leone,
Founders

Greenhaven Press anthologies primarily consist of previously published material taken from a variety of sources, including periodicals, books, scholarly journals, newspapers, government documents, and position papers from private and public organizations. These original sources are often edited for length and to ensure their accessibility for a young adult audience. The anthology editors also change the original titles of these works in order to clearly present the main thesis of each viewpoint and to explicitly indicate the opinion presented in the viewpoint. These alterations are made in consideration of both the reading and comprehension levels of a young adult audience. Every effort is made to ensure that Greenhaven Press accurately reflects the original intent of the authors included in this anthology.

Introduction

*"Children orphaned by AIDS are often consigned to a life
without hope."*
*—Kingsley Chiedu Moghalu, head of the Resource
Mobilization and Global Partnerships at the Global
Fund to Fight AIDS, Tuberculosis, and Malaria*

Throughout history, epidemics have devastated humanity.
During the fourteenth century, 25 million Europeans died
from the Black Plague, and more than 21 million people
died between 1918 and 1919 from the Spanish flu. In the
modern era the epidemic that has caused the most misery is
AIDS. Like the Black Plague, this disease has nearly destroyed a continent—in this case, Africa. As of late 2003, 29
million Africans were living either with AIDS or HIV, and
seven thousand Africans die from AIDS-related diseases
each day. The AIDS epidemic not only takes lives, but by
killing millions of young and middle-aged men and women,
it has created a particularly vulnerable population in an already troubled continent: AIDS orphans. Of the 14 million
AIDS orphans worldwide, 12 million live in Africa. According to the *British Medical Journal*, this already troubling
number could double by 2010, leaving one-third of all
African children orphaned. These children of AIDS victims
face often insurmountable economic and educational challenges. Finding ways to improve the lives of AIDS orphans
is critical if Africa is to thrive in the twenty-first century.

On a continent that is already impoverished, the loss of
parental income is economically devastating. As former
South African president Nelson Mandela observes, "AIDS
kills those on whom the society relies to grow the crops,
work in the mines and factories, run the schools and hospitals and govern countries." Since the affected nations do not
have the resources needed to build enough orphanages to
deal with the problem (for example, Zimbabwe has room for
only four thousand children in its facilities), these children
are either left homeless or sent to stay with other relatives.
Often these caretakers are elderly and too frail to work, so

orphans frequently begin working at a young age.

The need to enter the workforce at an early age is especially troubling because these children lack the education and skills to find safe and legal employment. Unfortunately, with their limited options, the jobs these boys and girls get are typically illegal and dangerous, such as prostitution and petty crime. AIDS orphans are frequently unable to attend school because public education in Africa is not free—schools charge fees, and uniforms are another significant expense. These costs can be even more prohibitive if the extended families in which the orphans live have other school-age children.

The lack of even basic schooling is devastating not only to these children but also to their countries. Girls who turn to prostitution or relationships with wealthy older men to earn money may become infected with HIV. Criminal lives can lead to early deaths. Thus, African nations not only lose the economic contributions of the parents who die from AIDS but also that of their children. In a speech before the Global Fund to Fight AIDS, Tuberculosis, and Malaria, Kingsley Chiedu Moghalu, who heads one of the fund's partnerships, observes: "The rise of AIDS orphans is breaking the generational transmission of knowledge that enables societies to survive, and will mire affected countries in poverty. The result will be the economic collapse of several societies."

Putting a stop to the crisis of AIDS orphans is a two-step process. First, African nations must find ways to reduce the spread of AIDS, including transmission between infected mothers and fetuses, so that fewer African children grow up without their parents and a new cycle of AIDS does not develop. Second, programs need to be developed so that the orphans have the opportunity to enjoy productive and healthy lives.

A variety of solutions to the AIDS epidemic has been offered in the twenty years since the disease first garnered worldwide attention. These responses include reducing infection rates by encouraging condom use and empowering women to find jobs so that they are not economically dependent on unfaithful husbands and therefore vulnerable to contracting AIDS. For infected parents, anti-AIDS drugs can extend their lives, which may allow their children to

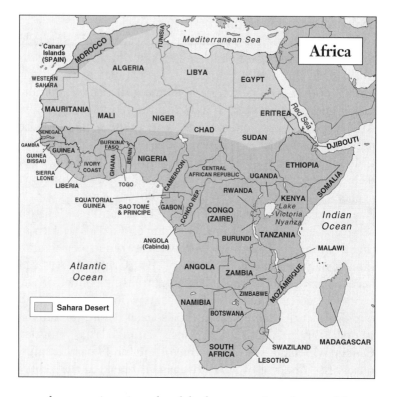

Africa

spend more time in school before entering the workforce. Anti-retroviral drugs that reduce transmission from pregnant women to fetuses have proven successful. However, access to anti-AIDS medicines in Africa has been thus far available to only a small percentage of the afflicted.

These solutions, however, do little to change the lives of already-orphaned children. African nations need to create programs that will help ensure better lives for these children. Economic assistance, such as providing grant money to families that take in orphaned children, is one way to improve lives. Another solution is to increase the role of local communities. For example, Laelia Zoe Gilborn, a researcher for the Population Council, suggests that teachers, guardians, and other adult volunteers should be trained to provide emotional support to children who are dealing with parental loss.

While these responses are important, arguably the best way to improve the lives of AIDS orphans is by making education more accessible. Some nations have started taking the necessary steps. For example, Mozambique's Ministry of Education developed a policy that exempts orphans from school fees. Child health researcher Alok Bhargava and former Ugandan government minister Betty Bigombe suggest in the *British Medical Journal* that African governments should subsidize the education of AIDS orphans. They argue, "In Ethiopia, Malawi, and Tanzania, about $40 per year per child would be sufficient to cover the costs of tuition, uniform, supplies, and transport." The authors also express support for larger subsidies (between $100 and $500) to help adolescents receive vocational training.

The plight of AIDS orphans is a tragedy that cannot be solved in the space of a year or two, though the above solutions should help improve the lives of the affected children. Nor is AIDS the only problem facing Africa; other issues include poverty, hunger, and the loss of native species. The authors in this book explore Africa's challenges and hopes in the following chapters: What Problems Does Africa Face? How Can the Spread of AIDS in Africa Be Reduced? What Policies Will Best Help Africa? How Can Africa's Wild Lands Be Preserved? Finding answers to these questions is critical if Africa is to prosper in the modern world.

CHAPTER 1

What Problems Does Africa Face?

Chapter Preface

Africa is beset by a number of problems, from political instability to an AIDS epidemic. One of its most long-standing woes is hunger. According to the United Nation's World Food Program, more than 40 million Africans are at risk of starvation. First recognized as a serious problem in the 1980s, the problem has shown few signs of vanishing.

Famine in Africa is a consequence of agricultural, socioeconomic, and political problems. The agricultural difficulties faced by African farmers include poor soil fertility, soil erosion, and inconsistent levels of rain. As a result of these problems, notes David Whitehouse in an article for *International Socialist Review*, "The soil, overworked in smaller and smaller plots by desperately poor farmers, produces only three to four months of a family's yearly grain requirement." Socioeconomic problems include urbanization; farmers are now fewer in number as more Africans move to cities, creating greater stress on inadequate supplies. Political realities that exacerbate hunger in Africa include a lack of democracy. David Masci, writing for *CQ Researcher*, observes that Zimbabwe's dictator Robert Mugabe "seized many white-owned and some black-owned farms [which has] shut down much of the country's once-thriving agricultural sector, helping to trigger much of the current famine."

Solutions to the problem of hunger are fraught with complications. Sending direct food aid from America and other Western nations may seem effective, but corrupt African governments often prevent the food from reaching their starving citizens. Other people suggest sending Africa seeds from genetically modified (GM) crops, which have been altered to ensure increased yields. This plan is widely criticized by environmentalists and scientists who question the health effects of GM crops and their impact on native plants.

A solution to Africa's famine that takes into account all of its causes may be found eventually, but for now hunger remains one of the continent's continuing problems. In the following chapter the authors debate other challenges facing Africa. Whether economic, political, or social, these problems have prevented Africa from prospering.

"Africa has not even entered the race for a share of the global economy."

Poverty Is a Problem in Africa

Godfrey Mwakikagile

Africa is the poorest of the six populated continents, with a per capita income and gross domestic product dwarfed by both Western nations and developing countries in Asia and Latin America. In the following viewpoint Godfrey Mwakikagile explains the causes of these economic problems. He contends that sub-Saharan Africa's endemic poverty should not be blamed on colonialism or imperialism, as was often suggested in the past, but rather on corrupt government officials, political instability, and a lack of basic technologies and infrastructure. Mwakikagile concludes that Africa's economic troubles are so vast that development will be a struggle. Mwakikagile is the author of numerous books on Africa, including *The Modern African State* and *Economic Development in Africa*, from which the following viewpoint has been excerpted.

As you read, consider the following questions:

1. According to Mwakikagile, which two sub-Saharan nations contribute more than one-half of that region's total gross domestic product?
2. In the author's opinion, why are people discouraged from investing in Africa?
3. What is the reason for the diminution of Africa's labor pool, according to the author?

Godfrey Mwakikagile, *Economic Development in Africa*. Commack, NY: Nova Science Publishers, Inc., 1999. Copyright © 1999 by Nova Science Publishers, Inc. All rights reserved. Reproduced by permission.

The modern African state has not done very well as a dynamic for social change because of its poor economic performance. It has been more static than dynamic because it has stifled individual initiative by dominating the economy, and also because in most cases it is a corrupt institution whose failure is writ large on the African economic landscape, telescoped into appalling statistics.

It is a sad commentary that the total gross domestic product (GDP) of all the 40 black African countries combined is dwarfed by that of a single country, Indonesia, which in 1965 was poorer than Nigeria, and was itself a colony that won independence roughly around the same time that African countries did: during the post–World War II era.

It is just as sad, probably even more so, when we look at the dismal performance of the black African countries from another perspective: more than half of their total GDP is contributed by only two countries, South Africa and Nigeria, whose combined GDP is $255.6 billion out of a total of $459.090 billion for the entire sub-Saharan region. That means a total of 38 black African countries—almost the entire region—have a combined gross domestic product of merely $203.49 billion (almost $203.5 billion), which is about a third of Indonesia's: a dismal statistic.

Speaking Out Against Corruption

But unlike in the past when it was fashionable for many Africans to blame colonialism and imperialism for almost all the problems their countries faced after they won independence, an increasing number of them today, especially those of the younger generation, insist on accountability within Africa itself; as they apportion guilt accordingly, instead of blaming colonialists and imperialists for the perpetual misery—due to tyranny and corruption, poverty and disease—hundreds of millions of Africans have to endure all their lives.

To these millions, independence is an abstract ideal which has yet to be translated into concrete reality, as they remain mired in poverty, and continue to be ravaged by disease, while billions of dollars in foreign aid and taxes paid by the toiling masses are being stolen and squandered by unscrupulous politicians and their cronies. It is clear where the problem lies: it lies within, not without. And the people of Africa are now beginning to speak up more and more against corrupt politicians, even risking their lives by doing so. As Ernest Aning bluntly states:

Millions of dollars are stashed away by corrupt leaders, their families and cronies. . . . The message is the same in Zaire, Tanzania, Kenya, Nigeria, Sierra Leone, Burkina Faso, Gambia, Ghana, etc. Development in Africa has stagnated over the years due to turncoat politicians and soldiers who have perpetuated themselves in office by manipulating the system.

We find ourselves asking: Where did all the good people in Africa go? . . . What happened to the foreign exchange and the loans given for development projects? Some of these funds find their way right back to donor countries, stashed in coded accounts.

Who do you call in Africa when you see waste and embezzlement? Nobody! Our courts are under the thumbs of the leaders. So what is the solution? Maybe we should all start to look around and ask questions about why there have been no additional hospitals, clinics, schools, roads, jobs or any change in our economic lives over the last two or three decades.

We should look at Thailand, South Korea, Indonesia, Singapore, Malaysia and all these countries that were just like us not too long ago. What are they doing, or better put what did they do, to change things? What did their governments do to achieve all these successes? . . .

In Africa, the average Joe goes into politics by any means possible to steal as much as he can. We've reached a point where the people can no longer be aloof. . . . (But) today, well-meaning citizens stand and watch because intimidation has become too real and life-threatening.

And as Maxwell Oteng, another African, also states:

A greater part of the blame on the present economic woes in our various countries should be apportioned to internal causes, especially bad political leadership. The Mobutus[1] had a very good chance to push us away from being perpetual producers of raw materials to producers of value-added goods which would have given us control over our products. Instead what did they do? . . . Until recent years, Malaysia was an agriculture-dependent primary producer like us, but it diversified the economy and encouraged local production of goods.

1. referring to the late Zairean president Mobutu Sese Seko

And in the words of yet another African, Simbowe Benson:

> Mobutu's hour of reckoning has finally come. And he deserves no sympathy! For three decades, he has run Zaire as his personal fiefdom, culminating in mismanagement and institutional corruption. Zaire is a rich country. . . . Now this rich nation has been reduced to penury while Mobutu and the Western business interests he fronts for have grown rich at the expense of the people. Laurent Kabila and his Alliance for Democratic Forces deserve our full support in their effort to unseat Mobutu and his sick regime.

Left Out of the Global Economy

Those are only three voices. But they express a collective sentiment shared across the continent. Corruption is destroying Africa. Even many investors, including local ones, are scared to invest in Africa, for a number of reasons of course, but corruption is one of them. African countries are also economically underdeveloped, technologically backward, and politically unstable. Any one of those reasons is enough to discourage investors. As Herman Cohen, the American assistant secretary of state for African affairs under President George Bush [President George W. Bush's father], stated:

> (Africa) does not provide the climate for investment and economic growth. Not only do foreign investors worry about the safety of what they're going to put in, but local people have the same problem. When I went to Ghana recently (1989), they asked why American investors aren't coming in. And I said, how come Ghanaian investors aren't investing? They said they're waiting for the Americans to show that we have confidence.

During the last several years, international trade, foreign investment and increasing technology have transformed the global economy and continue to improve the lives of hundreds of millions of people in the Third World. But this improvement has taken place mostly in Asia and in some parts of Latin America, alleviating poverty. Africa is the only underdeveloped region that has been almost completely left out. Hundreds of millions of her people have become poorer through the years, and there seems to be no way out of this vicious cycle of poverty and misery.

Political chaos, corruption, wrong economic policies, lack

Africa's Anemic Economies

Africa has 24% of the world's land and as many people as the Americas, but its economies are the world's poorest.

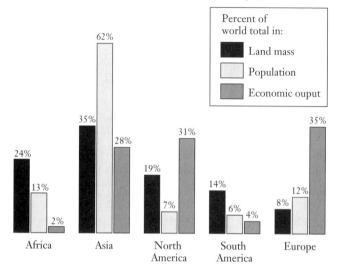

Milken Institute.

of infrastructure—poor transportation and communications and storage facilities—and a host of other problems including lack of skilled labor due to low levels of education, and poor health services which have led to diminution of the labor pool because of frequent and long-term illnesses; all those problems collectively are the reason why African countries are in the deplorable condition they are in today, an entire generation after independence.

Bypassed by Technology

In fact most of them were better off during the first decade of independence during the sixties than they are today. Besides the Congo and a few other hot spots, they had less chaos then than they do today, and they had more to eat then than they do today. Some of these countries even exported food during those days. Yet they had plenty left for the people to eat and sell on the domestic market. And almost all of them exported food decades before the sixties. As Dr. Robert Gardiner, the internationally renowned Ghanaian economist who was the first Executive Secretary of the UN Economic Commission for Africa, stated at the 15th Session of the UN Economic and Social Council in Geneva, Switzerland, on July 12, 1968:

Africa, Asia and Latin America were all net grain exporters thirty years ago, when the total grain outflow from these regions was taking place at an average annual rate of 11 million tons. In the 1940s, the developing regions became net importers; and by 1965, developing Africa was importing 4 million tons of cereals more than it exported.

Today, almost 40 years after independence, almost all African countries not only import a substantial amount of food; many of them depend on food donations from other countries for sheer survival. Even other developing countries sometimes donate food to Africa, although they are not rich themselves. But they are still better off than most African countries. Yet they were just as poor as their African counterparts a generation ago. Some were even poorer. Not only are they richer today; they are also far more technologically advanced than almost all the African countries. Even simple technology has bypassed Africa; and where such technology is available, it can still be a battle to get things done, as this case illustrates:

For years, customers could not call Kwabena Afari, a pineapple exporter, directly in Aburi, his hometown 65 miles north of here (Accra). His clients first had to call this city, Ghana's capital. Then someone here would call the Aburi post office. Then a post office messenger (from the Aburi post office) would go to Mr. Aburi's home (usually walking, or on a bicycle). If anything went wrong, and it frequently did, he might not receive the message for days. "Customers were complaining," said Mr. Afari, 46, who recently bought a cellular telephone. "My guy in Turin (Italy) got fed up. He said, 'I can't work with you any more. It is hard to communicate.'" Mr. Afari's struggles are an example of what ails sub-Saharan Africa. . . . As a great wave of trade and foreign investment transforms the global economy . . . sub-Saharan Africa has been left behind.

That is something Africans themselves admit. In fact things are worse than that. Africa has not even entered the race for a share of the global economy, which goes to the swiftest; those who attract foreign investors and have the upper hand in technical skills Africans' don't have, creating a climate conducive to foreign investment. As Lucia Quachey, head of the Ghanaian Association of Women Entrepreneurs, put it:

> It's not that we have been left behind. It's that we haven't even started.

Appalling Statistics

In fact Africa has fallen so far behind that it really has nowhere else to go but forward, even if it's at a snail's pace, while others are flying. Statistics tell the story, and it is a sad one through the years. They paint a gloomy picture of Africa's socioeconomic status, yet a realistic one. In its report entitled "ECA and Africa's Development, 1983–2008," the Economic Commission for Africa (ECA) has the following to say:

> In 1980, the average per capita income of the African region was only $741 compared with a per capita GNP of $9,684 in the industrialized countries. But this crude measure says little about the sad realities of life in Africa.

Then the report goes on to depict an even more appalling statistical profile of Africa's socioeconomic plight:

- 70 out of every 100 Africans are either destitute or on the verge of poverty.
- Only 1 in every 4 Africans has access to clean water.
- Of the 33 million people added to the work force during the 1970s, only 15 percent found remunerative employment.
- Per capita income has risen more slowly in Africa than in any other part of the world in the last 20 years.
- Africa's population is expanding at a rate of 2.8 percent annually, while food production is expanding at 1.5 percent.
- In 1980 Africa spent $5 billion importing 20.4 million tons of grain, excluding substantial freight costs.
- In 1980, the average African had 12 percent less home-grown food than in 1960.
- Africa's potential arable land is estimated at 4.2 acres per person, yet only 1.4 acres per person are currently being used.
- Africa's average food production per acre is about half of the world's average.

In his introduction to the report, ECA Executive Secretary Adebayo Adedeji said if the current trends continue for 25 years, which means until the year 2008, Africa's socioeconomic situation would be "horrendous." Sadly enough, we are almost there and, in many respects, Africa is no better off than she was back in 1983 when the ECA report was issued.

Nevertheless to avert the catastrophe the ECA, back then, called upon massive reforms across Africa's socioeconomic spectrum, and in international relations as well. To reverse the negative historical trends, the Commission called for the industrialized nations to live up to their commitment of devoting 0.7 percent of their gross national product to development assistance for African countries, a pledge made to other Third World nations as well; it also exhorted African nations to manage their own resources better in order to fuel an "industrial takeoff." Warning African countries about the devastating effects of their dependence on imported food, the ECA report recommended changes in agricultural pricing—which discourages African farmers and peasants from producing a lot of food since they are not paid much for it when they sell it on the domestic market; it also recommended changes in land-tenure practices. Both of those changes were recommended as an incentive to increased food production.

But the ECA report proposed nothing new in terms of solutions. However, in emphasizing the darker side of Africa's socioeconomic predicament, with grim statistics, the report left no doubt that Africa faces enormous problems just to be able to survive at the subsistence level, let alone develop.

"*Although poverty remains endemic, . . .
many governments in Africa are striving
hard to restructure their economies.*"

Africa's Economy Is Improving

Stephen Timewell

Although some African nations continue to struggle economically, the outlook for Africa's financial future is largely positive, Stephen Timewell contends in the following viewpoint.
He cites the success of debt relief programs and South Africa's
economic expansion as indications of a positive financial future for the rest of the continent. However, Timewell cautions
that famine and political instability in nations such as Nigeria
and Zimbabwe can lead to economic struggles. Timewell is
the editor of the financial magazine *Banker*.

As you read, consider the following questions:
1. According to Abdoulaye Bio-Tchano, what two factors
   does economic development require?
2. According to economic analysts, what is the minimum
   percentage of economic growth required to reduce
   poverty levels?
3. In the author's view, what is the core problem that
   affects Nigeria's economy?

Attitudes not only in Africa but also towards Africa are changing. While it is far too early to forecast glowing successes, there is enough momentum for genuine reform to signal a degree of optimism across the sub-Saharan region.

Although cynics may jeer, the [2002] meeting of African ministers at the New Partnership for African Development (Nepad) conference in Johannesburg called for equal treatment and internal economic solutions, not pleas for aid and concessions. Countries are beginning to face up to their challenges themselves and criticise the international community for unfair trade practices; and experienced financial institutions are beginning to seize the opportunities that are emerging.

Although poverty remains endemic, with nearly half of the population of the continent living on less than $1 per day, and HIV/AIDS has become one of the leading causes of death with about 28 million people affected, many governments in Africa are striving hard to restructure their economies.

Economic Reforms

"A generation ago it was fashionable to debate whether the state or the private sector should lead the way for economic development," says Abdoulaye Bio-Tchano, director of the IMF's [International Monetary Fund] African department. "Today, we know that development requires an honest, well-functioning state and a dynamic private sector. Many African governments have embraced this, and are now carrying out the reforms needed to boost private savings and investment, growth and employment."

In return for promises of reform, increased liberalisation, improved governance and the creation of a more enabling environment for the private sector, bankers say that Africa's leaders have been seeking more investment, debt reduction, more effective aid and improved market access, especially to the economies of the developed world. Although African growth rates outstripped the rest of the world [in 2001 and 2002], the global economic slowdown leaves the continent struggling for external support. According to the Institute of International Finance, private capital flows to Africa and the Middle East are forecast to fall this year to $9.2bn [billion], a mere 7.5% of total flows to emerging markets. And, contrary to popular perceptions, net official flows have declined since the early 1990s and are expected to be less than $20bn for the entire world [in 2001 and 2002].

Examples of Success

A closer look at the [African] countries that achieved positive [economic] growth rates during 1995–97 reveals that these countries also made progress in a number of other areas. Specifically, many countries were successful in:

> Reducing and containing inflationary pressures: more than two-thirds of the countries in the study group experienced either a decline in the average inflation rate or maintained average inflation at single digit rates.

> Increasing the ratio of domestic savings to GDP [Gross Domestic Product]: two-thirds of those countries that improved their growth performance also increased domestic savings as a percentage of GDP.

> Strengthening fiscal performance: two-thirds of the countries that raised their domestic savings ratios improved their overall fiscal balances.

> Increasing private sector investment: overall investment increased in sub-Saharan Africa during the period under study, but the private sector share in investment grew proportionately more.

Anupam Basu, *Economic Issues*, August 2000.

But, while the negative impact of the global recession and reduced capital flows cannot be ignored, there are positives coming out of Africa. "While at one time Africa's conflicts seemed to have been intractable, it appears as though peace is breaking out everywhere," notes Standard Chartered Bank's Africa economist Razia Khan. "Considerable progress has been made. Ethiopia and Eritrea are both emerging from war. Sierra Leone has had its first post-conflict election. Angola's civil war has ended, and promising peace negotiations are under way in the Democratic Republic of Congo, in Burundi, in Sudan and perhaps soon even in Somalia."

Along with changing political structures, the highly-indebted poor country (HIPC) debt forgiveness schemes are also proving their worth. Razia Khan explains: "Over the last decade, Mozambique and Uganda, early recipients of HIPC debt forgiveness, have both initiated economic reforms that have made a tremendous difference to their economies and show no signs of slipping. In fact, the promise of HIPC debt relief is expected to swell the ranks of Africa's strong reformers. Yes, it is true that HIPC alone is no panacea, and that declining commodity prices often mean that even the debt relief that is offered is insufficient. But the practice of putting in place the policies that are needed to attain HIPC debt forgiveness in the first place, the achievement of higher levels of external reserves, more spending on poverty alleviation, more balanced budgets and lower inflation are all factors that will contribute to growth in the longer term."

Three other countries, Burkino Faso, Mauritania and Tanzania, have also reached the completion point under HIPC and gained full debt relief. And a number of others have undergone assessments but have not completed, including: Benin, Cameroon, Chad, Ethiopia, The Gambia, Ghana, Guinea, Madagascar, Malawi, Mali, Niger, Sierra Leone and Zambia.

South Africa's Economic Expansion

The key to the continent is the performance of the larger economies, led by South Africa and Nigeria. Despite the slow global economy, South Africa has managed to achieve record trade surpluses on the back of the weaker rand [its currency]. This has led to an estimated 2.3% growth [in 2002] and a forecast 3.5% growth in 2003, but analysts suggest that this is still well short of the 6% needed to raise living standards and reduce poverty levels.

South Africa is seen as performing reasonably well although still seen as vulnerable on the inflation front and to any escalation in oil prices. Nevertheless, a stable political climate is [making] the country an increasingly attractive destination for foreign direct investment (FDI) and, with increased access to markets, the results are showing. South African exports to the European Union grew a further 11% [in 2001]; in effect exports are up 50% in two years.

This expansion has also been felt in the continent. South African banks and corporates are looking north and are expanding their African operations, either through acquisitions such as Nedbank's 40% stake in Equator Bank or Standard Bank increasing its already extensive branch network. Absa Bank and Standard are also moving into the retail arena as well as, like other South African banks, taking a larger share of the corporate market, which has largely been dominated by the international banking giants such as Citibank, Barclays and Standard Chartered.

South Africa's migration north is bringing a range of positive offshoots. Standard & Poor's [in November 2002] revised the outlook to positive from stable on Development Bank of Southern Africa. The bank is the government's primary vehicle for promoting infrastructure development in the country's municipal and utility sector and in the states of the Southern African Development Community.

S&P noted: "The outlook change on South Africa reflects the government's continued strong fiscal performance and ongoing improvements in the country's external position. Moreover, in addition to continuing to play a major role in South Africa's development policies, which ensures continued government support, the bank's contribution toward achieving development objectives for the African region as a whole is likely to grow over time."

Nigeria's Economic Struggles

Nigeria, Africa's most populous country, presents a different picture. Despite massive oil reserves, which account for 45% of GDP [gross domestic product] and 90% of exports, it is not the rich country its oil production of well over two million barrels a day would suggest. Economic growth has failed to keep pace with population growth, leaving the estimated 125 million Nigerians in 2001 with a lower per capita income ($282) than they had in 1980.

These figures, however, do not tell the full story: unofficial revenues are estimated at two to three times official totals, and [in 2002] oil revenues are expected to be well up because of higher than expected oil prices (more than the $18 a barrel budgeted for) and oil production well in excess of its 1.9mbd [million barrels per day] OPEC [Organization of Petroleum Exporting Countries] quota.

Besides oil and gas reserves, which are expected to triple by 2010, Nigeria has abundant natural resources, including tin, columbite, iron ore, coal, lead and zinc, and the agricultural potential to be food self-sufficient. The core problem, however, is the complex political system and the ethnic, regional and religious pressures that dominate it. After returning to civilian rule in 1999, the country now faces another round of presidential elections. . . .

While bankers such as Standard Chartered's Africa head Peter Sullivan are bullish about Africa's second largest market, with big opportunities in the corporate and wealth management segments, there are plenty of caveats and cautions. Godwin Oboh, managing director of Union Bank of Nigeria, the country's second largest bank, says: "If we can successfully hold elections, that will be the beginning of Nigeria's rising fortunes."

Forward and Backward

Another country with strong economic and banking potential is Kenya. It also faces elections due at the end of [2002]. It is expected to benefit from strong growth in east Africa coming from Uganda and Tanzania. The latest survey of foreign direct investment shows Tanzania as the third largest recipient of FDI in Africa [in 2001] after South Africa, with $6.6bn, and Morocco, with $3.3bn.

But, while many countries are making progress with cautious optimism in Ghana, for example, others are going backwards. The unexpected coup in Côte d'Ivoire in September [2002] leading to domestic instability is one example. And Zimbabwe faces a food emergency and is in its fourth straight year of contraction with GDP expected to fall by 12% [in 2002]. Africa may have its problems but many countries appear to be steering in a positive direction.

"In most [sub-Saharan African countries] democracy is a sham."

Africa Is Not Ready for Democracy

Marina Ottaway

African nations are not yet ready to establish democratic governments, Marina Ottaway asserts in the following viewpoint. She contends that current efforts at democracy have failed because African governments have not proven themselves capable of making major decisions, having been emasculated by international institutions, such as the International Monetary Fund, that set economic, education, and health policies. In order for African democracy to eventually be viable, Ottaway maintains, African states must be strengthened; such an improvement in African governments would also enable the continent to become part of the global economy. Ottaway is a senior associate at the Carnegie Endowment for International Peace, specializing in democracy and global policy issues, and a lecturer at Johns Hopkins University in Baltimore.

As you read, consider the following questions:
1. According to Ottaway, what percentage of Africans lives in nations that are considered free?
2. According to the author, why have African states always had difficulty engendering loyalty from their citizens?
3. What steps are required in order to strengthen African states, in the author's opinion?

In 1990, only three African countries had formally democratic systems. Now 43 of 48 sub-Saharan African countries have held multiparty elections. But this superficially rosy picture hides a much starker reality. In most of these countries democracy is a sham. Much of the continent's population lives in deeply troubled, even disintegrating states. In Africa today, stemming state decay is a more urgent task than building democracy.

Africans Lack Freedom

In 2001–2002, the Freedom House Index rated only nine countries in sub-Saharan Africa as free, 24 partially free and 15 not free. Only 13 percent of the African population lives in countries rated free. Five of the most populous countries, accounting for more than 40 percent of the continent's population, are shaken by internal conflicts, or teetering on the verge of disintegration. Nigeria, the Democratic Republic of the Congo, Ethiopia, Angola and the Sudan are unstable and divided countries, whose problems could affect entire regions.

Many explanations have been provided for these unhappy political conditions, including the colonial legacy, the arbitrary nature of African boundaries, poor leadership or the rise of "neopatrimonialism"—an ill-defined code word for the political ills that afflict the continent. Less discussed is the fundamental fact that without a functioning government capable of making major decisions, democracy does not have much meaning.

Granted independence by a fiat of international decision-making, rather than because they developed the administrative, financial and military capacity to govern and defend themselves, African states from the beginning had trouble either commanding the loyalty of their citizens or forcing them to submit to their power. From the outset, the state was less important for many Africans than immediate patrons, religious leaders or ethnic leaders. Today, the state is also less important than the international institutions and bilateral donors that impose policies and pay the bills.

When a country's macroeconomic policy is prescribed by the International Monetary Fund, its education and health policies are negotiated with the World Bank in the preparation of a Poverty Reduction Strategy Paper, and domestic and foreign nongovernment organizations have more influence on revenue spending than the government—as is the case for oil revenue in Chad—the election of a president and a Parliament have little impact on policies.

Creating Stronger States

Three sets of problems contribute to the present African predicament: the weakness of states, their lack of integration in the new international economy and their lack of democracy. Ideally, donors seeking to help African countries should address all three sets of problems at the same time. In reality, this is not possible because of funding and human resource constraints. So donors are forced to establish priorities.

The Difficulties of Nationality

One of the major difficulties for African democracy is the historical process that brought us together, forced us to live together and to constitute a Nation that we did not choose, while our own Nations came to be called ethnic groups. . . .

For example, a small country like Senegal comprises several nations which, prior to colonisation, had been subjected to domination and integration by various empires, but each time, they succeeded in maintaining their entities as nations. Some national groups are actually divided into several States. Others, while speaking the same language, belong to different historical nations. Thus the Ouolofs, who make up the majority of the population of Senegal, comprise various nationalities whose territories and last reigning kings are known: the Baoul, the Cayor, the Saloum and the Walo. The other nationalities (Diolas, Toucouleurs, Mandingues, Malinkes, Sereres etc.) also have their national peculiarities that differentiate them in terms of culture, physical structure and way of thinking.

Mazide N'Diaye, "Democracy in Africa," February 11, 2000.

Democracy should be the ultimate goal for African countries but it is not a good starting point. Rebuilding the state must come first, and the changes that would bolster the state are not those that would deepen democracy. Democracy requires the strengthening of parliaments and judiciaries and the curbing of the power of the executive. Strengthening the state requires building up executive agencies and the administrative apparatus. Indeed, without an increase in their capacity to control and administer the country, states will continue to disintegrate whether or not the government is elected or the judiciary is independent.

Without a clear improvement in their administrative and, in extreme cases, even military and police capacities, even democratic governments would not be able to promote their countries' integration in the global economy. The major beneficiaries of preferential trade measures, such as the U.S. African Growth and Opportunity Act, are those countries whose governments are able to guide entrepreneurs through the maze of implementation rules. Strong states like South Africa and Mauritius are already benefiting, while the changes make no difference to the Democratic Republic of the Congo or to Burundi.

Entering the Global Economy

Addressing the governance deficit by building up the capacity of administrative agencies is the most promising focus for helping African countries move forward. Africa needs stable states in order to become democratic. It also needs strong states in order to become better integrated in the global economy.

The reason is simple: Africa needs to become part of the global economy, but the global economy hardly needs Africa, except for raw materials it can already obtain. There is no "scramble for Africa" today. Rather, it is African countries that must scramble to integrate economically and politically, and that requires stable states and capable governments.

"Albeit 'thin' and elite-dominated, Africa's few democracies, . . . are still experiments worth preserving and extending."

Democracy in Africa Can Succeed

Richard Sandbrook

In the following viewpoint Richard Sandbrook acknowledges that although democracies in Africa can be considered "thin" (limited to the political sphere) and largely dominated by the elite, these new governments should be viewed as promising experiments that are worth continuing. According to Sandbrook, political liberalization began in earnest in the late 1980s and early 1990s, with almost all sub-Saharan African nations holding competitive national elections by 1999. Although he concedes that in many of these countries subsequent elections have been less democratic, he argues that no other alternatives have been proposed that offer as much hope to African nations. Sandbrook is a professor of political science at the University of Toronto and the author of *Closing the Circle: Democratization and Development in Africa*, the source of the following viewpoint.

As you read, consider the following questions:

1. What are some of the circumstances that led to Africa's democratic wave in the early 1990s, according to the author?
2. Why does Sandbrook disagree with the assertion that Western governments have considerable power over Africa's political processes?

Richard Sandbrook, *Closing the Circle: Democratization and Development in Africa*. London: Zed Books; Toronto, Canada: Between the Lines, 2000. Copyright © 2000 by Richard Sandbrook. Reproduced by permission of Zed Books, Ltd., and Between the Lines.

A strong authoritarian tendency emerged in the 1960s, the first decade of independence for most of the former colonies in Africa. The nationalist movements that had led their peoples to independence generally moved quickly to undermine or abolish the opposition parties. Control of the government gave the ruling group the patronage resources to co-opt opponents and extend and consolidate their support base. Control of the legal and coercive apparatus allowed government leaders to imprison opposition leaders (under preventive detention laws), limit the rights of assembly, free speech, and association, repress recalcitrant newspapers, and intimidate their opponents.

If the opposition did not "voluntarily" merge with the governing party (as in Kenya and Zimbabwe, for example), its parties were banned (as in Tanzania, Ghana, Guinea, and Niger, among others). [Political scholar] Robert Fatton vividly describes the common pattern: "The single party became the unique voice of the people, and the unique voice became the exclusive voice of the ruling groups, and soon the voice of the ruling groups became the voice of a unique individual. The nation was the party but the party was the undisputed and unchallenged leader. Thus started the descent of the one party into the cruel hell of dictatorship, privilege, praetorianism, and injustice." As popular disgust with the venality and arbitrariness of single-party states grew, governments usually responded with increased coercion. This growing governmental dependence upon the military set the stage for the wave of coups and countercoups that punctuated political histories from the mid-1960s.

Democracy was soon in short supply. Of the original forty-seven Sub-Saharan countries, only three—Mauritius, Botswana, and Gambia—retained multiparty democracy for twenty years or more. These three cases are atypical in their small populations (about one million inhabitants) and, with respect to the first two, economic prosperity. Senegal, a larger (nine million people) and less prosperous West African county, began a phased return to competitive party politics in 1976 under its poet-president, Léopold Senghor, and maintained this system, albeit under strain, into the new millennium. The only other country that holds some claim to prolonged multiparty rule is Zimbabwe since its independence in 1980; but this is a case of a one-party dominant system in which the incumbent president, Robert Mugabe, has brooked little opposition, constitutional or not.

A Wave of Democracy

Circumstances changed dramatically in the late 1980s, ushering in a democratic wave in the early 1990s. Economic depression in the 1980s discredited authoritarian governments. Programs of macroeconomic stabilization and liberalization sponsored by the International Monetary Fund (IMF) and World Bank levied heavy costs on the strategically placed urban workers and middle class, pushing them into opposition. Meanwhile, the joint pressures of economic contraction and stabilization programs shrank the patronage resources on which autocratic regimes had rested. Many countries were ripe for political change by the early 1990s. Urban demonstrations, riots, and strikes, and outbreaks of armed conflict or, in some cases, "terrorism," attested to the ferment in country after country. External developments gave impetus to domestic movements. The overthrow of Eastern European tyrants in 1989 encouraged democracy movements everywhere, and the new U.S. and British enthusiasm for democracy following the Cold War deprived "friendly" African dictators of their external supporters, leaving them vulnerable to opponents who espoused the principles of democracy.

The pace and geographical scope of democratization were remarkable. Of the forty-seven Sub-Saharan countries, twenty-nine staged a total of fifty-four elections in the period 1989–94. Election observers declared more than half of these elections free and fair. Voter turnout, moreover, was relatively high, averaging 64 per cent. In fourteen cases, elections initiated a peaceful transfer of power to a new president. Political liberalization also blossomed in most of the countries that did not hold competitive elections, usually entailing the legalization of opposition parties, the launching of private newspapers, and the right of opposition parties to hold rallies. By 1999 only a handful of countries had failed to convene competitive national elections. Holdouts such as Somalia, Sudan, and the Democratic Republic of the Congo (Kinshasa) had already succumbed to state collapse or civil war. Second sets of national elections began in 1995; but in ten of the sixteen countries that had held these campaigns by the end of 1997 the quality of the elections declined relative to the earlier set. Opposition boycotts of elections were common.

The Phases of Democratization

Democratization, though, is a contested term, and calls for careful definition. I usually employ the formal or conventional usage, in which democratization is a process involving two phases. An *electoral transition* begins with a crack in, or breakdown of, an authoritarian regime. This phase ends with the holding of a "free and fair" election and the installation of a new government. To be free and fair, an electoral system must reflect certain core civil and political liberties: freedoms of movement, association, and expression and the right of all adult citizens to vote and hold office. The second, lengthier phase involves the *consolidation of democracy:* the growth of widespread support for the formal institutions of democratic competition and governance. Clearly, democracy will have little meaning if, between periodic electoral contests, rulers govern autocratically. The consolidation of democracy therefore involves the internalization of rules governing the exercise of power on a day-to-day basis, as well as of rules underpinning free and fair electoral contests. Political leaders, to achieve legitimacy, must come to accept horizontal accountability between elections—that they are answerable to the legislature, courts, oversight agencies (such as an auditor-general), and even the media, for their actions. Perhaps only Mauritius and Botswana approximate consolidated democracies in this broad sense, although opposition leaders in both countries would dispute this assertion.

I also employ a second, more informal sense of democratization. This refers to the activities of "popular" or grassroots movements to empower groups of citizens by asserting their rights or enhancing their control over their lives. The Greenbelt Movement in Kenya, for instance, mobilizes rural women for the seemingly prosaic task of planting trees; yet this particular organizational process has also shown broader implications for rural power relations. Although the term can be used to refer to both of these formal and informal processes, here, unless otherwise mentioned, democratization refers to the former.

Democracy in Nigeria

The successful election in Nigeria and the subsequent peaceful civilian-to-civilian transition of government last May [2003] demonstrated that democracy has indeed taken root in the country. For [Nigeria's] administration, the renewed mandate is a clear endorsement of our leadership vision and policy priorities by the electorate. Thus emboldened, we have since announced the . . . far-reaching reform programs that, by the grace of God, should consolidate the gains of the previous four years, thoroughly sanitize our social system and firmly set Nigeria on the path of sustainable development and prosperity.

Olusegun Obasanjo, *Origins*, October 9, 2003.

How should we evaluate the authenticity of democratization in this formal sense? Skeptics contend that, whatever its theoretical merits, democracy in contemporary Africa is largely a sham. For critics on the left, Western-assisted democratization fosters only "low-intensity democracy" or "consensual domination," which functions merely to legitimize open-market economies (which is part of "structural adjustment") and divert the masses from a more radical democratization of social and economic life [according to W.I. Robinson]. "Polyarchy [Western-style formal democracy in the emergent global society," according to W.I. Robinson, "has as little to do with democracy as 'socialism' in the former Soviet bloc had to do with socialism." Issa Shivji (1990), a foremost African critic of liberal democracy, also makes this general argument. Far from heralding major political reforms, he claims, multiparty democracy will, at best, merely widen the recruitment of political elites while the vast inequities and the old practices of cronyism and clientelism will continue as before. Western governments and agencies assist African democratization in order to reassert capitalist hegemony and encourage market-based development by disciplining capricious dictators. John Saul, another critic of liberal democracy and advocate of popular democracy, correctly argues that "much of the literature on 'Third World' democratization has come to turn on a very narrow reading of democratic possibility." This reading is rooted, Saul suggests, in the notion of "polyarchy" (as popularized by [Robert] Dahl 1971) in which democracy is reduced to a procedural exercise—periodic competitive elections in which organized groups vie for the popular vote in a context of protected civil liberties. Democracy is thus "thin," restricted to the political sphere and involving the replacement of one section of the elite by another. What is required instead is movement towards a "popular democracy." This notion is defined variously: by Saul as synonymous with democratic empowerment, by Shivji as a political regime based on the expansion of popular participation via people's organizations, and by Robinson as a "dispersal throughout society of political power" that can be used "to change unjust social and economic structures."

African Democracy Is Not a Sham

Albeit "thin" and elite-dominated, Africa's few democracies, I contend, are still experiments worth preserving and extending. It is inaccurate to characterize democratization as a foreign imposition, or even as solely an affair of the elites—unless that elite is construed to include such underprivileged elements as Ghana's famous "verandah boys," for example. Dictators have often yielded to genuine democracy movements, which sometimes draw upon a long tradition of struggle against oppression. That Western powers have supported African democratization largely because it suits their own economic and strategic objectives is true, and their efforts to promote Western-style democratic governance may well bolster the hegemony of the emerging global political and economic order. But the story does not end there. Scholars often criticized the U.S. and other Western governments for supporting friendly dictators during the Cold War. Should we then fault these same governments when they have dumped dictators in favour of elections and due process—especially when this external support is avidly sought by Africa's democratic activists? Consider also the phenomenon of unintended consequences. Critics assume that Western governments can exercise considerable control over political processes in Africa. This proposition is dubious. Although outsiders may wish to promote market-friendly governments and divert radical grassroots tendencies, history suggests that they possess only limited leverage in achieving these goals.

Then too, just because African democracy can accurately be characterized as thin, it is not, therefore, a sham. Most mainstream evaluations also highlight the shortcomings of these experiments. In light of Africa's hostile structural and historical conditions, one would not expect otherwise. Yet if certain democratic regimes have decayed into "pseudo-democracy," others have not; and new democracies are always a work in progress, not a final outcome. When regimes are in flux, it is premature to judge them definitively.

Even a low-intensity democracy may be preferable from the viewpoint of ordinary citizens to its practical alternative—which in Africa's conditions is probably renewed dictatorship. None of the critics offers more than the vaguest notion of what the more desirable alternative, popular democracy, would concretely entail, or how it might be achieved. Even Saul accepts that the prospects for popular democracy are bleak.

"Lawlessness is a trade-off for whites living in Africa."

Prejudice Against Whites Is a Problem in South Africa

Alec Russell

In the following viewpoint Alec Russell contends that South African whites face continual violence in the wake of granting political power to black South Africans. He asserts that whites view the robberies, rapes, and murders committed against them by black Africans with an air of defeatism, believing them to be acceptable trade-offs for being allowed to stay in Africa. Russell also argues that whites, including those who supported the end of apartheid, are largely assumed to be guilty of racism. He concludes that South Africa faces a bleak future if its black citizens continue to victimize whites. Russell is a writer for the British magazine *Spectator* and the author of *Big Men, Little People: Encounters in Africa*.

As you read, consider the following questions:

1. What scene in the book *Disgrace* does Russell find most telling?
2. What is the "Bloemfontein syndrome," as explained by the author?
3. According to Russell, how did the president of Uganda startle South African politicians?

Alec Russell, "The Price of Staying On," *Spectator*, vol. 283, November 6, 1999. Copyright © 1999 by The Spectator. Reproduced by permission of The Spectator.

The world's unofficial murder capital [Johannesburg] is at its most glorious at this time of year. The jacaranda is cloaking the suburbs in purple; the heady sweet smell of syringa is in the air; the first rain clouds of the summer are rumbling over the veld. So I had no hesitation the other evening when an old Afrikaner friend suggested a jog to wipe away the cobwebs from the Cape Cabernet of the night before. This was my first visit to Johannesburg since I left 18 months ago after five years as the *Daily Telegraph*'s correspondent. It felt excellent to be back.

Within a few 100 yards we had touched on everything from the prospects of the England cricket tour to the pulse of the rainbow nation [a nickname for South Africa]. We were almost back home when my eye was caught by a familiar sign—The Singing Fig—one of my favourite restaurants in my Jo'burg days. 'The Singing Fig!' I exclaimed nostalgically. 'How is it doing?' 'Oh, fine.' There was a pause. 'Well . . . they were cleaned out recently. Ten guys with guns walked in—or was it five? They took everything.' I grunted as if to say, 'Oh, of course, that old story', and we ran on, turning our thoughts to the Springboks' [cricket team] chances of holding on to their crown.

The Power of Race

South Africans of all races have long since learned to inure themselves to the daily threat of violence. Take the protagonist of *Disgrace*, J.M. Coetzee's Booker–winning novel, a white academic adrift amid the chaos of the new order. Much has been made of what his daughter says after she is gang-raped. 'What if that is the price to pay for staying on?' she asks her father. 'They [the rapists] see me as owing something. They see themselves as debt collectors, tax collectors. Why should I be allowed to live here without paying? Perhaps that is what they tell themselves.' More telling is the scene when the lecturer is sidelined by the forces of political correctness at a disciplinary hearing. With a mixture of arrogance and defeatism he despairs of a fair trial and gives up the fight. It is a sequence that rings all too true these days for many whites. It was always clear that race would be a political trump-card in the new order.

Enemy number one since the end of white rule has been the Democratic party, the descendant of the old liberal opponents of apartheid. In South Africa's parallel universes they are the only trenchant critics of the ANC [African National Congress], or 'reactionary racists', depending on your point of view. But it is not just the old liberals who are taking a pounding.

Attacks Against Whites in Zimbabwe

Swarms of blacks calling themselves "war veterans" are now squatting on approximately 1,000 (some reports put the figure at 700) commercial farms, egged on by [Zimbabwe's president Robert] Mugabe's denunciation of white farmers as "enemies of the people." Arriving in government-supplied convoys, they camp out on private property, demand food and drink, and intimidate farmers and their black employees. Many admit they are being paid by the government. Often roaring drunk and brandishing clubs and knives, they sometimes make the farmers' wives and daughters dance for them or sing songs praising Robert Mugabe and the [political party] ZANUPF. At their worst they kill, burn, rape, and loot. It is a miracle that so far only three farmers have been murdered, but many have been beaten, held hostage, or forced to sign documents transferring ownership of their farms to the occupiers.

George Kimble, *American Renaissance*, June 2000.

Now it is the turn of the white left-wingers, who backed the revolution, to pay for their pigmentation. The day of my run through Johannesburg's suburbs, a long-running inquiry into Helena Dolny, the widow of the communist leader, Joe Slovo, was drawing to a close. As managing director of the Land Bank, she stood accused of granting herself a large salary increase. But there was another element to the Dolny affair: a former colleague had accused her of racism.

If Ms Dolny is a 'racist', then you might as well begin with the premise that South Africa should kick out its four-million-odd whites and start again. Joe Slovo would have laughed off the charge with a loud expletive but in 1999 you have to be more careful. A new concept of 'subliminal racism' is in vogue, and lies behind the Promotion of Equality Bill which was tabled in parliament [in October 1999]. 'Equality courts' are to be set up. Guilt is assumed. Those accused of 'racism' will have to prove their innocence.

Open Season on Whites

Ms Dolny was cleared of racism, but the lesson was clear: it is open season. Every white manager goes to work wondering which black colleague is going to point the accusing finger. Some still stick their heads above the parapet and say what they think is right rather than what is 'correct'. But for most, in particular those in the media whose commitment to the 'dream' is on daily show, it is simpler to lie low.

My visit coincided with the funeral of [Tanzania's first president] Julius Nyerere. Day after day the newspapers printed encomiums. There was barely a mention of his socialist one-party state in Tanzania, the thousands of imprisoned dissenters, and the economy he bankrupted. A rare article that did touch on such inconvenient facts qualified them with the suggestion that to dwell on them was the mark of a Western mindset.

It is the 'Bloemfontein syndrome', one senior white journalist told me. Lt Sibusiso Madebula did not get much airtime overseas when he walked into his army base outside Bloemfontein and shot dead seven white colleagues, before killing himself. His spree coincided with a massacre in a Baptist church in Texas, a much more compelling, CNN-style tale. But it shook white South Africa to the core. It was a reminder of the anger still simmering over three centuries of humiliation. It was a cue to do your job and hold your tongue.

South Africa still has, of course, by far and away the world's greatest density of moaners. President Thabo Mbeki has resisted the temptation of penalising white purses. As [former South African president] F.W. de Klerk says in his autobiography, 'In the country club lounges the ladies continued to play bridge and sip tea.' And as for the 'strugglers', as white antiapartheid activists were known, it is hard not to sympathise with Mondli Makhanya, a leading black journalist, when he took them to task for whingeing. 'Whites left must still learn that the struggle was not an investment' ran the headline over his piece.

A Bleak Future

However, by lumping all whites together, the post-apartheid regime may be sowing the seeds of its own destruction—as well as falling into the same trap as the Nationalists. And the added tragedy is that South Africa is taking this path as most of the rest of the continent moves in a different direction. Yoweri Museveni, the President of Uganda, has no great love for whites but he knows that they need to be wooed, if only for their money. He startled MPs [members of parliament] in Cape Town's parliament a few years ago when he told them that 'blaming colonialism is like a drunken man blaming someone who steals his hat'.

I spent my penultimate night on a farm in the bush some 250 miles north of Johannesburg. My hosts were attacked [in 1998] and were lucky to survive. But they are staying because they believe that lawlessness is a trade-off for whites living in Africa. It is a bleak vision. Unless the race card is put back in the pack, it will become reality.

| "*[Black South Africa's] position of
subordination in the racial hierarchy is
systematically reinforced.*"

Prejudice Against Blacks Is a Problem in South Africa

James M. Statman

Despite the end of apartheid, blacks continue to experience
prejudice in South Africa, James M. Statman maintains in
the following viewpoint. According to Statman, this oppression can be seen in the ways whites behave condescendingly
toward blacks, such as when they use the term "girl" and
"boy" to refer to black workers. Oppression can also be seen
in the lesser economic status of most black South Africans.
However, notes Statman, white South Africans are blind to
their own failings and unable to recognize the racial inequality besetting their country. Statman is a political psy-
chologist and writer.

As you read, consider the following questions:

1. How does the author react to the claim that no one is in
   Johannesburg in December?
2. In the view of white South Africans, according to
   Statman, what is validated by violent crime?
3. According to a census report cited by the author, what
   percentage of black South Africans were unemployed in
   1996?

James M. Statman, "The Shape of the Shadow: Mapping the Dimensions of
White Amnesia and Denial in Postapartheid South Africa," *ReVision*, vol. 22,
Summer 1999. Copyright © 1999 by the Helen Dwight Reid Educational
Foundation. Reproduced by permission of the Helen Dwight Reid Educational
Foundation, published by Heldref Publications, 1319 18th St. NW, Washington,
DC 20036-1802.

Despite the fall of the apartheid order, the advent of a new black elite and a black-led government, and five years into its new democracy, South Africa is a divided society deeply polarized along the old fault lines of race. Given its cruel history of 350 years of white domination, that fact alone is hardly surprising. But what is for me far more shocking and unexpected is the extent to which, even now, much of white South Africa remains inured to its own privilege, unable and unwilling to recognize the fundamental social, economic, and moral realities of its own society. After a transition to democracy characterized by breathtaking magnanimity on the part of the black majority, after more than three years of devastating Truth and Reconciliation Commission testimonies documenting the appalling parameters of apartheid inhumanity, white society seems resolutely unwilling to acknowledge those truths or to respond with caring and generosity. Better to forget the past, deny the present, and to use a favorite phrase, "get on with our lives.". . .

A Destructive Paradigm

Of course white South Africa would prefer to maintain its affluent life style, economic domination, and sense of cultural superiority; hence its persistent snide criticism of life in the new South Africa and its historic blindness to the failings and depravity of the old order. But if it is to avoid an ultimate confrontation with the masses of black poor—whose celebrated patience, if one is to judge by the prevalence of violent crime, may be finally reaching its limit—would it not be in the self-interest of white South Africans to demonstrate a concern for improving the well-being of the majority? What keeps the white nation entrapped in a paradigm so blatantly destructive to the "other" and to itself?

Living and working in South Africa, I exist within the bubble of affluence and superiority, of shared discourse and delusion, encapsulating most whites. Even as an outsider, within this enveloping context of separation and gross inequity, I struggle to maintain a moral compass, to retain a critical awareness of all the ways, large and small, in which the assumptions, the world view, and the easy perks of privilege begin to narrow my perspective. Perhaps one small example may convey a sense of those daily dilemmas. Each December when Johannesburg's restaurants and cinemas seem almost empty and radio personalities casually remark that "no one is in town," I have to remind myself that despite visual evidence, that is simply not true. For while many white families may indeed be enjoying a summer holiday by the sea in Cape Town or Durban, most in metropolitan Johannesburg, surely the millions in Soweto and Alexandra, in the urban slums of Hillbrow and the semirural shacks of Orange Farm, have not departed for carefree vacation retreats. For the white residents of the northern suburbs, for the English language radio announcers taking their own world as the norm, the naturally given, any realities outside this particular existence seem hardly worth imagining or acknowledging—thus the narcissism of the powerful.

After the enormity of apartheid crimes, after the "miracle" of South Africa's transition to democracy, why berate the white community over matters that seem so relatively trivial? While black South Africa is no longer exposed to subjugation through organized, sanctioned state violence, through the violence of coercion, its position of subordination in the racial hierarchy is systematically reinforced through just such apparently small, innocent acts of social and linguistic positioning that together create a tapestry of domination through a kind of symbolic violence. It is here, through the power to control the meaning, the labeling, and the interpretation of everyday events, that white South Africa continues to exercise its prerogative of superiority. It is here, through myriad small acts and judgments, that the metapolitics of refined racial oppression becomes actualized. Live in South Africa for a short while and the list, the catalogue of interpersonal atrocities that you witness, begins to seem inexhaustible: the insistence that African names are unpronounceable and that blacks must therefore assume a Western name, like Nelson or Winnie; the reference to adult maids and gardeners as "girl" and "boy"; the directive air of superiority and condescension; the rudeness; the insulting asymmetrical use of first names; acting as if the "other" is invisible or stupid.

That symbolic oppression is manifest at two levels. In terms of concrete interaction between individuals, the slight, the small insult or indignity, makes its point, achieves its instrumental end, even as it inflicts its interpersonal wound. On the communal level, it reinforces the hierarchy of white and black, making clear who has the authority over the other. But it does so not simply by achieving its concrete objective, such as having the "other" carry the bundle or roundly scolding the "other" for making a simple mistake, but more important, by demonstrating who is in charge, who has the power to control and define meaning. In that way even the small interactions give covert evidence of far greater meaning.

Racial Disparities

Basic Demographics*

	Whites	Blacks	Mixed
Total population	4.43 million	31.12 million	3.60 million
Number of households	1.48 million	6.53 million	741,206

Jobs

	Whites	Blacks	Mixed
Employed	1.85 million	5.68 million	1.12 million
Unemployed	89,066	4.20 million	299,231
Earn $400 or more monthly	1.55 million	1.40 million	420,311

Sanitation

Number and % of households

	Whites	Blacks	Mixed
Flush toilets	1.47 million (99%)	2.21 million (34%)	590,000 (80%)

Telephones

Number and % of households

	Whites	Blacks	Mixed
Home telephone/ mobile telephone	1.31 million (89%)	740,783 (11%)	321,849 (43%)

Home Lighting

Number and % of households

	Whites	Blacks	Mixed
Electricity	1.47 million (99%)	2.85 million (44%)	619,454 (84%)
Candles	0	2.46 million (38%)	83,205 (11%)

* Not included in the three major population groups are Indians, Asians, and others unspecified, totaling 1.4 million people and 301,876 households.

Statistics South Africa, 1998.

And so the macropolitics of race becomes actualized on the microstage of the usual, the uneventful, the normal. And in the repetition of those little morality plays, those tiny demonstrations of the social order, all must collude. As much as everyone somehow understands the deeper meaning and significance of what is being said or acted, all must act as if they do not notice. White and black must pretend that the interactions are only being performed in the realm of the concrete. The lessons of power are then relegated to the realm of the shadow.

Some symbolic aspects of white domination become manifest in the broad public arena as statements of racial ideology, as for example in letters to the editor, newspaper columns, or talk show call-ins. Those are sites where the white world view and the racialized chit-chat of cocktail parties and barbecues become externalized and then consumed as self-affirming validation. Here it is common to find that despite centuries of oppression and only five years of black-led democracy, blacks are held responsible for the wretchedness of their communities and treated to sanctimonious lectures about the importance of education and hard work. It is as if apartheid barriers to black education and the underpaid toil of black miners, farm workers, factory workers, and maids were suddenly erased from the white communal memory bank. Faced with such external evidence of black laziness or incompetence and of their own communal superiority, whites fatalistically warn themselves of how bad things will be once blacks take over operation of the formerly fabulous white-led institutions. It is an appalling exercise in self-aggrandizement.

The public pronouncements of white communal discourse articulate a more or less coherent framework or explanation for why things are as they are, encapsulating and affirming the appropriateness of the everyday rules of racial interaction. Although there are numerous exceptions, by far most interactions between black and white South Africans occur in the highly stratified atmosphere of the work or service environment. Notwithstanding the significant if modest increase in the number of black managers and professionals, most black South Africans' positions on the ladder of employment status, as maids and gardeners, check-out clerks, waiters, or laborers, still typically require subordination to the whites with whom they interact, constantly reinforcing and naturalizing the old racial hierarchy.

Different Encounters

But there are also other, quite different, symbolically important sites and styles of real and imagined interaction between
whites and blacks, encounters that, while at least partially in-
congruent with the practice and ideology of white domination, become subsumed within its world view. Much more
than the change of government, it is the fact and threat of violent crime that creates a nexus for a symbolically different,
hierarchical encounter. Here the tables are turned, the duali-
ties of baas and servant reversed and exchanged for those of
victim and perpetrator. Violent crime assumes a unique place
in white discourse. As understood in the white nation, crime
serves to validate the very separation, inwardness, sense of
moral superiority, and domination that, through the exercise
of raw power, violently position blacks in the position of infe-
rior other. It matters little that blacks even more than whites
are themselves the victims of such violence. The violent crime
demonstrates the inferiority, if not of Africans as biological
entities, then at least of their barbaric, archaic culture, reify-
ing the necessity of white vigilance and social control. Fear of
harm by the "other" is thus construed to justify, as nothing
else can, the "preemptive" violence inflicted upon them.

And so white South Africa condemns itself to its self-
imposed quarantine, imprisoned not only by its history, its
culture, and its material circumstance, but more so by its
self-perpetuating shared illusions, grandiosity, fear, and in-
ability to comprehend a world beyond itself. In its fortress of
fortune, infected with the DNA of colonial privilege, it continues to replicate deeds of interpersonal and communal oppression, regardless of how dysfunctional, with only the
forms and language updated to fit the sanitized requirements of modern democratic sensibility.

Proof of Inequity

The struggle between rich and poor . . . is not merely a
struggle over work, property rights, grain, and cash. It is also
a struggle over the appropriation of symbols, a struggle over
how the past and present shall be understood and labeled, a
struggle to identify causes and assess blame, a contentious effort to give partisan meaning to local history. [James Scott,
Weapons of the Weak]

On 20 October 1998, two years after "the night of the count," Census 1996 was revealed to President [Nelson] Mandela and to the nation. The first national census in a democratic South Africa, it was awaited with great anticipation in a land where the validity of such research was historically subordinated to the political mythologies of the ruling party. As knowledge is power, so the knowledge historically presented through censuses was supportive of ongoing white empowerment and domination. Over the years, blacks were systematically undercounted and data from the ostensibly independent black homelands were excluded from consideration. But this time it was to be different; there was to be an inclusive census conducted with professional competence and scientific rigor.

Census 96 does seem to deliver what the *Johannesburg Star* in its headline termed the "harsh facts of a land still divided." And so we learn some particular numerical facts of life in the new South Africa. We learn that in October 1996 more than 40 percent of the black population was unemployed, as compared with less than 5 percent of the whites; that more than one-quarter of employed blacks earned 500 rand per month or less, at this moment roughly $90, as compared with less than 4 percent of whites; that 65 percent of the employed whites earned more than 3,501 rand per month, as compared with only 6 percent of blacks; that over one million blacks and about 900 whites live in squatter settlements; that about one-quarter of the black population over age twenty has had no formal education; and that 2.8 million black households rely on pit latrines, compared with 3,900 white households. And on and on it goes, enumerating the specific, quantitative details of racialized inequity. . . .

Understanding Reality

Like their black counterparts, on a personal level many white South Africans are warm, bright, funny, creative, energetic, self-deprecating, and helpful, the very kind of people whom I find extremely likable and attractive. Yet blinded by fear and the narrowest of self-interest, haunted by an extraordinary sense of victimhood, trapped by their communal sense of entitlement and superiority, with few exceptions they repeatedly fail to grasp more than token opportunities for mutuality and genuine engagement. South African whites need to look beyond the bounds of their own sheltered environments to begin to understand the realities of life for the majority of their fellow citizens and to appreciate and take some responsibility for how white success has been, and to a significant extent remains, predicated on black oppression and disadvantage. If they cannot do so and do so soon, the specter that haunts the South African miracle may indeed turn terribly ugly.

Periodical Bibliography

The following articles have been selected to supplement the diverse views presented in this chapter.

George B.N. Ayittey — "Zimbabwe's Tyrant," *Wall Street Journal*, March 6, 2002.

William Boyd — "In Africa, War Is What They Know," *New York Times*, August 28, 1999.

Gedahlia Braun — "South Africa, 1999," *American Renaissance*, August 1999.

Joel Carpenter — "Mandela's Miracle," *Books & Culture*, September/October 2000.

Anthony Daniels — "Big Men, Big Corruption," *National Review*, August 11, 2003.

Sunday Dare — "A Continent in Crisis," *Dollars and Sense*, July/August 2001.

Economist — "Africa's Democratic Joys and Tribulations," June 5, 1999.

Nick Greenslade — "My Zimbabwe," *In These Times*, January 6, 2003.

Isebill V. Gruhn — "Human Rights Abuses in Africa," *Human Rights Review*, October–December 1999.

David Masci — "Famine in Africa," *CQ Researcher*, November 8, 2002.

Joseph Siegle — "A Tale of Two Africas," *Los Angeles Times*, July 13, 2003.

Moctar Teyeb — "A Call for Freedom," *Tikkun*, July/August 2000.

Cynthia Tucker — "Nigeria Offers Ray of Hope in the Bad News That Is Africa," *Liberal Opinion Week*, March 15, 1999.

G. Pascal Zachary — "Africa in Agony," *In These Times*, June 26, 2000.

CHAPTER 2

How Can the Spread of AIDS in Africa Be Reduced?

Chapter Preface

The spread of AIDS in Africa is arguably the worst health crisis in the world today. As of late 2003, 30 million Africans were infected with the HIV virus or had full-blown AIDS, and more than 15 million Africans have died from AIDS-related diseases. These deaths and illnesses have left children orphaned, wrecked Africa's economy, and sent average life expectancies in some Africa nations plummeting.

One group that AIDS has left especially vulnerable is African women, who comprise 58 percent of the infected population. AIDS and HIV disproportionately affect African women because they hold little power in sexual relationships. Because they are often considered to be their husband's property, many African wives lack the authority to refuse sexual intercourse with their husbands or demand that they wear condoms, even if the wives have reason to suspect they have been unfaithful. Teenaged girls often engage in sex acts with older and wealthier men for much-needed money, increasing the likelihood that these young women will become infected. Prostitutes are also vulnerable to the virus if their clients refuse to use condoms.

Many observers of the AIDS crisis contend that the best way to reduce the spread of AIDS in Africa is by empowering women, although common African mores may make that difficult to achieve. *Village Voice* reporter Mark Schoofs, who wrote a series on the African AIDS crisis, cites a Zambian study that found that women who complete their education are four times less likely to become infected. This lower rate of infection is due to the fact that educated women become sexually active at a later age and are more likely to be financially independent, thus alleviating the need to marry or prostitute themselves. Sexual education, in which girls learn about abstinence and the need to avoid unprotected intercourse whenever possible, is also critical. Schoofs also cites a South African program in which peer educators teach prostitutes about the importance of condoms and provide strategies to convince their customers to wear them. However, notes Schoofs, these and other solutions cannot be wholly successful without male support. He writes, "[The peer-education project] . . . highlights the daunting challenges of HIV education: Some men will offer as much as five times the going rate for unsheathed, flesh-to-flesh sex."

The AIDS crisis in Africa presents daunting challenges to health care workers and others concerned with Africans' well-being. In the following chapter the authors consider several ways to reduce the spread of AIDS in Africa. While empowering women through education is one approach, more than one solution will need to be implemented in order to stop the virus's onslaught.

"Lifesaving HIV/AIDS-drug cocktails . . . [are] vastly out of the reach of all but a small handful of the growing African population with HIV/AIDS."

Anti-AIDS Drugs Need to Be More Affordable

Robert Weissman

In the following viewpoint Robert Weissman asserts that actions by U.S. pharmaceutical companies have made drugs that fight AIDS unaffordable to African AIDS patients. He argues that these companies' refusal to allow less-expensive generic equivalents to be sold in Africa is an immoral and cruel policy that is worsening an already serious problem. Weissman further contends that drug companies can develop new medicines for use in Africa without seriously affecting their profits. Weissman is the editor of *Multinational Monitor* magazine and the codirector of Essential Action, a corporate accountability group.

As you read, consider the following questions:
1. What is compulsory licensing, as explained by Weissman?
2. In the author's opinion, how do drug companies exaggerate the costs of developing new drugs?
3. According to Weissman, what is the cruelest claim made by the pharmaceutical industry?

One in seven Kenyans and one in four Zimbabweans have HIV/AIDS. In South Africa, 22 percent of adults are HIV positive. South African life expectancy, which stood at 59 years in 1990, is projected to be less than 40 years by 2010.

In the United States, existing treatments enable many people with HIV/AIDS to live relatively healthy lives. But lifesaving HIV/AIDS-drug cocktails cost about $12,000 a year in many African countries—vastly out of the reach of all but a small handful of the growing African population with HIV/AIDS. So, for virtually everyone in Africa, an HIV/AIDS diagnosis is a death sentence.

With more than 22 million people in Africa diagnosed as HIV positive, the AIDS pandemic is a public-health disaster of epic proportions, crying out for a dramatic treatment-delivery effort.

A Pharmaceutical Controversy

But the U.S. drug makers have not assisted such a humanitarian project. Instead, the U.S. drug makers and their allies in the federal government have sabotaged the modest steps that African countries, particularly South Africa, have taken to make essential medicines available to their people.

The primary focus of controversy has been a provision of South Africa's Medicines Act that empowers the government to undertake parallel importing and compulsory-licensing policies.

Compulsory licensing enables countries to instruct a patent holder or other exclusive rights holder to license the right to use its patent to another party. South Africa might issue a license on a patented HIV/AIDS drug manufactured by Bristol-Myers Squibb to a local producer. The South African maker would then manufacture the drug for sale in South Africa under a generic name, and it would pay a reasonable royalty to Bristol-Myers Squibb on each sale.

By introducing generic competition, compulsory licenses drive prices down. In the case of pharmaceuticals, compulsory licensing can lower the price of medicines to consumers by 75 percent or more.

Parallel imports involve imports of a product from one country and resale, without authorization of the original seller, in another. South Africa might purchase a Glaxo Wellcome HIV/AIDS drug in France, priced lower than in South Africa, and then resell it in South Africa.

Multinational pharmaceutical companies object to parallel imports and compulsory licensing, however, since they may lose profits—especially if the practice is imitated in the United States.

A Bullying Effort

A large grouping of multinational pharmaceutical companies has sued in South African courts to block implementation of the controversial provision of the Medicines Act. And the industry successfully has enlisted the U.S. government to undertake a massive bullying effort to get South Africa to repeal the provisions.

A report from the State Department says, "All relevant agencies of the U.S. Government have been engaged in an assiduous, concerted campaign to persuade the Government of South Africa to withdraw or modify" the Medicines Act provisions that give the government the authority to pursue compulsory licensing and parallel-import policies. Vice President Al Gore has overseen this effort as cochair of the U.S.–South Africa Binational Commission and has raised the issue repeatedly with South Africa's former deputy president and now current President Thabo Mbeki. Gore's office claims that he has actually been a moderating influence on U.S. policy. The United States has withheld trade benefits and threatened trade sanctions as punishment for South Africa refusing to repeal the provisions of its Medicines Act that offend the multinational drug companies.

There is absolutely no legitimate purpose for this immoral, cruel policy that works to deny access to essential medicines to the sick and dying. The United States maintains the policy solely to satisfy drug-industry demands.

Both compulsory licensing and parallel imports are permitted under the international trade rules established by the General Agreement on Tariffs and Trade, or GATT, and administered by the World Trade Organization, or WTO.

The GATT's Agreement on Trade-Related Aspects of Intellectual Property, or TRIPS, contains the international rules the WTO enforces on intellectual property (patents, copyrights and trademarks). The pharmaceutical industry heavily influenced the TRIPS agreement negotiations, and many public-interest advocates generally believe the TRIPS agreement tilts toward corporations.

But whatever the TRIPS agreement's biases, it specifically permits compulsory licensing and allows for parallel imports. Parallel imports are permitted without limitation, and the agreement elucidates the precise and generally reasonable rules that countries must follow to do compulsory licensing. South Africa repeatedly has stated its commitment to undertake compulsory licensing only in a TRIPS-compliant manner.

Access to AIDS Drugs in Africa

Should pharmaceutical companies be doing more to help solve the problem of AIDS in sub-Saharan Africa?

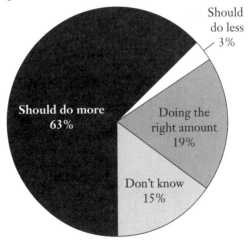

Should
do less
3%

Should do more
63%

Doing the
right amount
19%

Don't know
15%

Henry J. Kaiser Family Foundation, May 2000.

Parallel importing and compulsory licensing are common practices around the globe. In the United States, compulsory licenses regularly are issued on products ranging from pesticides to pollution-control devices to computer-processing chips.

U.S. officials and pharmaceutical-industry representatives at times admit the legality of compulsory licensing and parallel importing under the WTO. But they contend nonetheless that compulsory licensing and parallel importing would unfairly impinge on the companies' intellectual-property rights.

These claims ignore, however, that compulsory licensing is part of the intellectual-property system—it is one of the many limitations on patent rights, and patent holders know this when they receive a patent. Under WTO compulsory-licensing rules, companies will receive reasonable royalties when a patented invention is used.

Suspect Claims

The industry and its apologists also argue that the high cost of research and development, or R&D, requires that companies be given freedom to charge whatever they want. But it is unreasonable to give a blank check to anyone who controls life-saving technologies. And the drug makers' claims about the threat to their R&D budgets is suspect for several reasons.

First, the drug companies routinely exaggerate the costs of developing new drugs. They rarely note that governments often finance the key R&D costs of important new drugs. In the case of HIV/AIDS, for example, the two leading candidates for compulsory licensing are the drugs AZT and ddI, both of which were developed at the National Institutes of Health partly at U.S. taxpayer expense. Both drugs have generated huge profits for the drug companies.

Second, although this most profitable of industries—one that spends far more on marketing, advertising and administration than R&D—regularly claims that government efforts to restrain prices will undermine R&D. Prior initiatives to constrain price gouging (for example, Medicaid price controls) in fact have not translated into lower R&D expenditures.

Third, because compulsory licensing will increase company sales (as it lowers prices), it may not harm industry earnings, or may hurt earnings less than initially appears to be the case.

Fourth, African markets are paltry for the multinational drug companies—2 percent or less of the global total (developing countries' share is about 10 percent). Lower revenues from developing countries, should they occur, would not affect company R&D efforts or profitability to any significant extent.

Finally, there is a moral issue: Should people with HIV/AIDS in poor countries be denied available treatments so the companies can earn higher profits? Neither compulsory licensing nor parallel imports involves the companies selling products at a loss.

More Questionable Arguments

With AIDS activists raising the temperature on the debate over drug-company activities in Africa, the industry has pulled out a new set of arguments. Drugs are not a cure-all, they argue curiously; addressing HIV/AIDS requires better health-care systems. This surely is true—but it hardly is an argument against making desperately needed medicines more affordable.

The drug-company lobbyists also assert that parallel imports and compulsory licensing will not lower drug prices sufficiently to make them widely available. But these policies in fact will enable many more Africans to obtain drug-cocktail therapies; they also will lower prices for drugs that treat AIDS-related opportunistic infections, enabling many to avoid preventable suffering, and will make more affordable short-course therapies (for example, to prevent mother-to-child HIV transmission).

In the cruelest claim of all, some industry representatives or allies suggest that making HIV/AIDS drugs available to Africans poses the risk of creating drug-resistant strains of the disease. The premise of this argument is that Africans with HIV/AIDS today should die quietly so that others, someday or perhaps somewhere else, may live. To understand how extreme a claim this is, remember that more than 22 million Africans are HIV positive.

"The solution to the development of drug resistance due to patient difficulty in adhering to the often-complex AIDS drug regimens is not denial of drugs, but rather interventions to improve adherence," says Peter Lurie, a physician associated with Public Citizen's Health Research Group. "In fact," Lurie . . . told the House Government Reform subcommittee on Criminal Justice, Drug Policy and Human Resources, "high drug prices are one of the causes of nonadherence, as poor patients may take partial drug courses to save money." Moreover, "such interventions have had substantial success with tuberculosis in developing countries." And the deny-treatment argument also ignores the many benefits that lower medicine prices will have for treating opportunistic infections, mother-to-child transmission and other HIV/AIDS-related problems that do not raise the specter of drug resistance.

The alternative to compulsory licensing and parallel importing, according to the drug companies, is charity. But while some companies have made donations of drugs or joined with the UNAIDS program in small treatment efforts, charitable initiatives do not have anywhere near the scope or broad effect of South Africa's Medicines Act.

It certainly is true that the HIV/AIDS crisis requires a more multifaceted response than policies designed to lower drug prices—prevention programs, destigmatization of people with HIV/AIDS and improvement in health-care systems are among the vital changes urgently needed.

But access to treatment is indisputably a critical element of what needs to be accomplished, and it is the area where the drug companies could and should play a positive role. Instead, they shamefully have hindered efforts to make medicines available to the sick. Even if AIDS activists' pressure soon forces a change in U.S. industry and government policy on South Africa, the rest of Africa and the world will remain vulnerable to their bullying.

"Without adequate health care networks to monitor their distribution, potent new medicines are worse than useless; they're dangerous."

Making Anti-AIDS Drugs More Affordable Could Worsen the Crisis

Siddhartha Mukherjee

Many people have suggested that the best way to reduce the spread of AIDS in Africa is by making medicines that fight the HIV virus more affordable. In the following viewpoint Siddhartha Mukherjee maintains that such a response could backfire and ultimately worsen the threat of AIDS. According to Mukherjee, anti-AIDS medicines are dangerous if they are not taken properly, as the HIV virus can quickly mutate in a patient taking low dosages and become resistant to the drugs. He suggests that pharmaceutical companies can lessen the danger by paying to develop the medical infrastructure needed to ensure that the drugs they sell are properly administered. Mukherjee is a clinical fellow at Harvard Medical School.

As you read, consider the following questions:
1. According to the author, how much money does it take to treat one person with anti-HIV drugs for a year?
2. What percentage of AIDS patients has HIV strains resistant to the drug AZT?
3. In Mukherjee's opinion, why is HIV so deadly?

Siddhartha Mukherjee, "Take Your Medicine," *New Republic*, July 24, 2000.

[July 2000's] international AIDS Conference in Durban, South Africa, was a spectacularly glum affair. While angry protesters outside the conference railed against greedy pharmaceutical companies, delegates inside recited dismal statistics about the plague, each more alarming than the last. In South Africa, approximately one in ten adults is HIV-positive; in Africa as a whole, AIDS now takes three times as many lives as the next most common cause of death. Of all the depressing numbers, there was only one that health officials felt confident about changing any time soon: the $15,000 it currently costs to treat just one person with anti-HIV drugs for a year.

The reason is something called "tiered pricing" or "equity pricing," a concept that UNAIDS, the United Nations agency dealing with AIDS, began promoting recently and that elicited considerable excitement in Durban. . . . Under the scheme, Western pharmaceutical companies, like Merck and Glaxo Wellcome, would set different prices for drugs in rich and poor countries. The same pill—say, AZT—could be sold for $4 in New York but only 40 cents in Johannesburg. With tiered pricing, Africans could finally afford the anti-HIV medicines they desperately need, and drug companies could still turn a reasonable profit.

New Medicines Can Be Dangerous

A great idea? Actually, no—at least not by itself. What the enthusiasts seem not to realize is that without adequate health care networks to monitor their distribution, potent new medicines are worse than useless; they're dangerous. Consider Russia's recent experience with anti-tuberculosis drugs. In the 1990s, physicians in the former Soviet Union unleashed a torrent of anti-tuberculosis drugs on the population. The drugs were great, but the patients taking them weren't adequately supervised; in many hospitals, as many as 50 percent of patients strayed from the prescribed regimen. Soon, upwards of five percent of patients in some Russian clinics began to exhibit a strain of tuberculosis completely resistant to all drugs. Subsequently, millions of dollars had to be spent to contain the deadly strain. As Dr. C. Robert Horsburgh, a public health expert from Boston University, . . .

An Impossible Expense

It is absurd to suppose that Western medicine will solve the problem in Africa. Even if the drugs were provided free, you would need, by African standards, impossibly expensive support facilities to monitor the effects of treatment. One major London teaching hospital has a budget of about £20 million a year to treat 2,000 patients with HIV. This compares with a per capita healthcare budget for all medical problems of $20 per person per year in Uganda, which is far from the poorest of African nations.

Spectator, April 21, 2001.

---

warned in the *Journal of American Medicine*, "The genie of multi-drug-resistant TB [was] irreversibly out of the bottle."

The HIV genie is even more ominous. HIV's secret—one reason the wispy virus is now a continent-hopping Goliath—is that it mutates rapidly, quickly becoming resistant to drugs. If anti-HIV drugs are not taken properly—a missed capsule here, a forgotten pill there—a low level of viral reproduction continues within the body. And the viruses brewed while the anti-viral medicines are still present in a patient's system can be especially lethal, as they are selected to carry mutations that render them resistant to the original drug. Even in the United States, where an excellent health care network monitors most drug regimens, about ten percent of patients already harbor HIV strains resistant to AZT, the most common anti-HIV drug. And if such potent drugs are dumped unsupervised on Africa—where health care networks cannot afford to be as vigilant—then a virulent, drug-resistant strain of HIV may emerge very quickly and could even boomerang back to the West.

Creating an Infrastructure

Fortunately, there is an alternative to the solution hyped . . . in Durban. Since the safety of anti-HIV drugs depends on a country's health care infrastructure, pharmaceutical companies could pay to develop in Africa some of the infrastructure necessary to make sure their anti-HIV drugs are taken properly.

Why would drug companies do something so altruistic? Because it's not altruistic at all. After all, drug companies can only squeeze profits out of Africa by selling Africans their anti-HIV drugs over a long period of time. Right now, with about 22 million Africans infected with HIV, the demand for anti-viral drugs seems inexhaustible. But, if a viral strain immune to a company's drug emerged, the drugmakers would no longer have medicine Africans wanted to buy. Even worse, the resistant virus might spread into more profitable Western markets. Only by making an investment in health care infrastructure—and thus preventing drug-resistant strains of HIV from coming to life—can a pharmaceutical company ensure that its cash-cow drug isn't rapidly made worthless by new mutations.

Glaxo Wellcome, at least, seems to understand this. In May [2000], the company announced it would enter an unusual collaboration with UNAIDS to make sure its discounted anti-HIV drugs would be sold only in selected areas—places that "address[ed] the health care infrastructure and drug distribution aspects" and where there was "access to safe and effective ongoing treatment" for HIV. Glaxo also agreed to foot some of the bill for building these infrastructures through direct training and technical support of AIDS advocacy groups.

No one can be sure the Glaxo-UNAIDS scheme will work, because nothing like it has ever really been tried. There isn't much precedent for such public and private collaborations actually creating safe environments for selling discounted drugs. But, then again, there isn't much precedent for a recalcitrant virus infecting whole swaths of an entire continent. HIV is so deadly because it is enormously resourceful, crafty, and even creative. To defeat it, we will have to be as well.

"HIV/AIDS prevention efforts that do not include condoms as an option are incomplete and ultimately ineffective."

Condoms Are the Best Way to Fight AIDS

Nada Chaya and Kali-Ahset Amen

The leading cause of death in sub-Saharan Africa is AIDS, a disease that has killed more than 11 million Africans. The best way to fight the spread of AIDS in Africa is through widespread condom promotion and distribution, Nada Chaya and Kali-Ahset Amen assert in the following viewpoint. They argue that condoms are cost-effective and are the only proven way to prevent the transmission of HIV during sexual intercourse. The authors conclude that AIDS prevention programs that ignore the importance of condoms are destined to be ineffective. Chaya and Amen are employees of Population Action International, a policy advocacy group that is committed to providing universal access to family planning information and slowing population growth.

As you read, consider the following questions:
1. What are the "ABCs" of AIDS prevention, according to the authors?
2. How much does it cost to save a life each year through health education and condom distribution, according to a study cited by Chaya and Amen?
3. As noted by the authors, what percentage of AIDS transmission in Africa occurs via heterosexual intercourse?

Nada Chaya and Kali-Ahset Amen, *Condoms Count: Meeting the Need in the Era of HIV/AIDS*. Washington, DC: Population Action International, 2002. Copyright © 2002 by Population Action International. Reproduced by permission.

AIDS has already killed more than 20 million people worldwide. More than 40 million other people are today living with HIV infection, almost half of whom are women and a full third are young people aged 15–24. AIDS is the leading cause of death in sub-Saharan Africa, the fourth leading killer worldwide, and HIV, the cause of AIDS, continues to spread in every corner of the globe. No country is immune.

And yet infection by HIV can be avoided. All that is required is for all people everywhere to be given the information, education, skills and full access to the ways they need to protect themselves and others. Male and female condoms are an essential component of such efforts and expanding and improving condom promotion and distribution are absolutely vital to success in the fight against the spread of AIDS.

Condoms Save Lives

The fact that condoms can save lives is indisputable. It is also a fact that a great many people in every country have no alternative to condom use for protecting themselves or their sexual partners, wives or husbands from infection. Prevention efforts that do not include condoms are therefore incomplete and will ultimately be ineffective.

Although the promotion and distribution of condoms have increased significantly since the onset of AIDS, the need for *both* promotion and distribution still far outstrips the resources committed. It is estimated that a minimum of 8 billion condoms would have been needed in 2000 in order to achieve the kind of access required for significant reductions in the rate of infection and prevalence in the developing world and Eastern Europe. Donors provided just 950 million condoms that year, less than one-eighth of the number needed.

And while more developing country governments are allocating resources for prevention, national commitment remains inadequate. . . .

Supplies are, of course, only one part of the challenge in addressing poor reproductive health. This is particularly true with regard to the fight against HIV/AIDS, which requires significant changes not only in public policy, but also in individual attitudes, behaviors and in societal norms. Addressing poverty and the roots of gender inequities is key to such change.

To be effective, HIV/AIDS prevention programs must include a range and mix of interventions tailored to the specific needs of various groups and localities. The range must include promotion of the "ABCs" of prevention: abstinence, being faithful to one's partner, and condom use by the sexually active. And the mix of interventions must always include condoms—a most basic reproductive health technology that provides dual protection from infection and pregnancy. The international community, especially donor nations and institutions, must act quickly to mount large-scale comprehensive prevention efforts that strongly support promotion and distribution of condoms.

Failure to act is already having tragic consequences, particularly in sub-Saharan Africa where [in 2001] 2.2 million people died of AIDS and 28 million currently live with HIV/AIDS and where, in high prevalence countries, at least a third of boys now aged 15 will die of AIDS.

These horrifying statistics for Africa presage the future for other regions and countries unless preventive action—including widespread condom promotion and distribution—is immediately intensified. Despite the hold that HIV currently has on sub-Saharan Africa and, increasingly, on the world, we may one day look back upon this time as a moment of opportunity, when concerted prevention efforts could have made—or did make—a huge difference.

Why Condoms Are Effective

Some 14 thousand people a day become infected with HIV and the vast majority of these infections are sexual. Yet sexual transmission of HIV can be avoided through the practice of safer sex. Despite this fact, HIV continues to spread mainly because not enough people are practicing safer sex. Abstaining from sex, mutual monogamy between uninfected sexual partners, and the correct and consistent use of male and female condoms are the only existing options for avoiding sexual infection. It is therefore essential that everyone have access to the information and tools that enable them to have safe and responsible sexual relations and to negotiate safer sex, including condom use.

The condom is the only technology available for protection from sexually transmitted HIV. It is scientifically undisputed that the transmission of HIV during sexual intercourse can be prevented when condoms are used correctly and consistently. Nonetheless, condom use is still much too low, despite decades of promotion for use in the prevention of sexually transmitted infections (STIs)—including, since the early 1980s, HIV—and significant increases in distribution and availability. Insufficient use is due to many factors, among them generally low levels of awareness, poor availability and accessibility, especially for young people, misinformation, and the stigma attached to condoms.

Condoms in the Congo

Condoms are highly effective in preventing HIV transmission, but they entail costs—not only the money and time spent buying condoms, but potential inconvenience and embarrassment and, for some people, reduced pleasure. Reducing these costs will encourage more people to use condoms and lead to lower rates of HIV transmission. In Kinshasa, Democratic Republic of Congo, a program that offered sex workers free condoms, treatment for other sexually transmitted diseases, counseling, and group discussions had impressive results. A mere 11 percent of the sex workers had used condoms on an "occasional" basis before the program; afterwards, more than two-thirds reported using condoms on a "consistent" basis. The incidence of HIV—the number of new cases over time—dropped by two-thirds. At the same time, mass marketing of highly subsidized condoms—known as "social marketing"—in Kinshasa increased the willingness of clients to use them. Sixty developing countries now have condom social marketing programs, both for prevention of sexually transmitted diseases and HIV infection and for family planning.

Martha Ainsworth, *Finance & Development*, March 1998.

Condom use is especially important for individuals at higher risk of infection, including men who have sex with men, sex workers and their clients, injecting drug users, migrant workers and others who are obliged to spend long periods away from their regular sexual partners. However, there are people everywhere who cannot adopt an alternative method to condom use for protecting themselves or others such as those whose sexual partners are infected by HIV but also, and most obviously, the women and men forced by their circumstances into sex work. They must use condoms every time they have sex because they have little or no choice.

In those places where HIV prevention efforts have been successful in reducing prevalence and infection rates, condoms have played a key role. There are many documented cases illustrating the positive effects of condom promotion and increased use, including in Thailand among sex workers and their clients, and among young men in Brazil and India.

Effective and Affordable

Condoms are a simple and affordable yet life-saving technology. They can be easy to use, do not require medical supervision, and can be distributed through schools, places of employment, bars, and other public venues, as well as health care facilities. Where they are available, both male and female condoms are increasingly affordable through free or subsidized distribution.

Prevention efforts that include condoms are highly cost-effective. It is obviously better to prevent HIV infection now than to bear the human, societal and financial costs of illness and its treatment and care later. According to a study by the University of California at Berkeley, interventions to control STIs among urban sex workers that include health education and condom distribution are the most cost-effective interventions and cost just US$3.50 per life saved per year. Somewhat more costly, at US$19.49 per life saved per year, were voluntary counseling and testing interventions (VCT) that included condom distribution to program participants. In comparison, treatment with the generic form of anti-retrovirals and monitoring the patient's therapy using a directly-observed therapy (DOT) regimen cost US$1,033 per year.

Whatever its initial entry point into a population, HIV eventually spreads through sexual transmission. Although in its initial stages the epidemic may spread mainly through unsafe blood and injecting drug users, HIV inevitably spreads within the general population as a sexually transmitted infection. The most heavily affected countries are those in the later stages of the epidemic's development.

More than 80 percent of HIV transmission is now heterosexual in Africa, where the epidemic has been established the longest. The Caribbean is the second most affected region and the vast majority of infections in Central America and the Caribbean are the result of unsafe heterosexual sex and frequent partner exchange among young men and women. In parts of South America, which has a more diverse epidemic, men having sex with men account for as much as 70 percent of infections. In Asia and the Pacific, most HIV infections still result from unprotected sex between commercial sex workers and their clients and between men, in addition to injecting drug use, but this pattern will likely change if the epidemic develops further.

Preventing Other Diseases

Where curable sexually transmitted infections exist, so does HIV. Worldwide, over 300 million new cases of curable STIs occur annually, with a regional distribution similar to that of HIV. Infection with an STI increases a person's risk of acquiring HIV, especially for a woman. If detected, many STIs can be successfully treated, but delays in seeking treatment, shortcomings of STI services, and the reality that many infections are asymptomatic, mean STIs too often go untreated. Correct and consistent condom use, and other behaviors to limit exposure to infection, can prevent sexually transmitted infections, especially HIV. The prevention and treatment of STIs can therefore be effective in reducing HIV incidence, particularly where HIV prevalence is low but that of STIs is high.

While societies and their governments may view the promotion of condoms as a means to reduce rising rates of HIV prevalence, the main reason for promoting condoms is to offer to individuals one of only three possible means of protection from sexual infection by a 99.9% fatal virus (only rabies is more deadly than HIV). HIV/AIDS prevention efforts that do not include condoms as an option are incomplete and ultimately ineffective.

> *"Abstain and be faithful' is the human and Christian way of overcoming HIV/AIDS."*

Condoms Are Not the Best Way to Fight AIDS

Southern Africa Bishops

Traditional sexual values, not the promotion and distribution of condoms, is the only way to end the AIDS crisis in Africa, bishops from South Africa contend in the following viewpoint. The bishops claim that condom use is immoral, sends the wrong message about love and sexuality, and may even spread the virus because condoms are not always effective. The bishops argue that reducing the spread of AIDS requires abstaining from sexual intercourse before marriage and then remaining faithful to one's spouse. They maintain that by following the lessons taught by Christ and his apostles, Africans will protect themselves from AIDS. This viewpoint was originally a statement issued following a meeting of the Southern African Catholic Bishops' Conference, in which bishops from South Africa, Botswana, and Swaziland participated.

As you read, consider the following questions:

1. According to the bishops, what message does condom use send?
2. In the authors' opinion, what should married couples do if one spouse is infected with AIDS?
3. How is AIDS a sign of the times, according to the authors?

Southern Africa Bishops, "Message on the HIV/AIDS Crisis," *Origins*, vol. 31, August 16, 2001, pp. 199–201. Copyright © 2001 by Southern African Catholic Bishops' Conference. Reproduced by permission.

W̶e the people of southern Africa find ourselves in the middle of a great crisis in our nations caused by HIV/AIDS. Many people despair when they are stricken with HIV/AIDS because they feel rejected and sometimes are rejected by their families and communities. Some even commit suicide. In this desperate situation we, the Catholic bishops of southern Africa, bring a message of hope to all who are living with this killer disease:

Do not despair—you are not abandoned by Christ nor by us. When you find yourself in a hopeless situation on account of AIDS, Jesus, your brother, remains right next to you and never abandons you. We encourage your families and communities to accept you with love and to stand by you. We urge them not to abandon you but to continue Christ's mission of mercy, compassion and love. The church loves you, welcomes you and reaches out to you in many ways.

We have a message for our nations, the youth and married couples.

Condoms Are Not the Answer

Many people and especially governments promote condoms for preventing AIDS. This is a matter of deep concern for us in the church.

The bishops regard the widespread and indiscriminate promotion of condoms as an immoral and misguided weapon in our battle against HIV/AIDS for the following reasons.

- The use of condoms goes against human dignity.
- Condoms change the beautiful act of love into a selfish search for pleasure—while rejecting responsibility.
- Condoms do not guarantee protection against HIV/AIDS.
- Condoms may even be one of the main reasons for the spread of HIV/AIDS.

Apart from the possibility of condoms being faulty or wrongly used, they contribute to the breaking down of self-control and mutual respect.

The promotion and distribution of condoms as a means of having so-called "safe sex" contributes to the breaking down of the moral fiber of our nations because it gives a wrong message to people. What it really says is this:

- "It is all right to sleep around as you like even if you are still young—as long as you do not contract HIV/AIDS."
- "There is no need for training yourself in self-control."
- "There is no need to prepare yourself to be faithful to a future spouse."
- "It is all right to use another person for selfish pleasure."

What undermines the morals of our countries?

- It is lack of self-control and lack of respect for others.
- It is unfaithfulness and irresponsible sexual behavior.
- It is loose living, which destroys human dignity—*ubuntu*—and self-respect.

This is our conviction as Catholic bishops of southern Africa. We proclaim our message loud and clear, a message which will strengthen again the moral fiber of our countries:

"Abstain and be faithful" is the human and Christian way of overcoming HIV/AIDS.

Abstain from sex before marriage and be faithful to your spouse in marriage—this is the answer, which Christ gives us. With his help we will overcome AIDS and build up a new, happy and healthy South Africa, Botswana and Swaziland.

Message to the Youth

Dear young people, we are well aware that you are searching for real love, happiness and meaning in your lives. God says, "I am offering you life or death, blessing or curse. Choose life, then, so that you and your descendants may live." (Dt. 30:19).

Make sure you choose life by accepting God's way.

Do not allow yourselves to be misguided by people who show you the wrong way by offering you condoms. Abstain from sex before marriage, and be faithful to your spouse in your future marriage: This is the way Christ shows us.

We often hear people saying, "Condoms save lives, and therefore they should be promoted."

Our answer is, "If we follow Christ's way, we shall save far more lives and encourage people to grow in self-control and responsibility for others."

Dear young people, you should not say: "It is impossible to abstain." You must prove to yourselves that abstinence is possible and that lust is not love. There are many groups of young people who help one another in their struggle to live chaste lives. There are groups such as Youth Alive which promote "education for life" through workshops and programs inspired by the mottos "True Love Waits" and "Choose Life." Yes, it is difficult to abstain, but it is not impossible with God's help, which we obtain through prayer. Do not listen to people who say, "You will go mad if you do not have sex!" In fact you will be very healthy in mind and body.

Not a Fool-Proof Solution

The condom is not fool-proof protection either against pregnancy or HIV. It has a failure rate of 12 to 18 percent in preventing pregnancy. Some studies even show a failure rate of up to 30 percent. . . .

Even the most "modern" of societies with long experience in contraception aren't exemplary in the proper use of condoms. Witness the United States, where leaders of value-free sex education and promotion of contraception and abortion among her young people have not exactly brought about a decreased incidence of teenage pregnancies, much less a decline in AIDS cases. For that matter, witness Thailand.

Orestes Monzon, *HLI Reports*, January 1997.

To young people who are living with AIDS:

We encourage you to speak up openly and help your companions to avoid the disease. In this way you will truly become promoters of life. You are continuing the mission of Christ, who said, "I came so that they may have life and have it more abundantly" (Jn. 10:10).

We call on young men:

• Respect girls and young women, and relate to them without making sexual demands of them. St. Paul says, "God wills you all to be holy. He wants you to keep away from sexual immorality" (1 Thes. 4:3).

Message to Married Couples

We make a strong appeal to all married couples:

Husbands and wives, remain faithful to each other as you promised on your wedding day. In this way you proclaim God's faithful love for us.

In your difficulties, our God, who is faithful, will never abandon you. Keep in contact with God through prayer and listening to his word. We encourage you to support one another in your struggle of life.

There are couples where one of the parties is living with HIV/AIDS. In these cases there is the real danger that the healthy partner may contract this killer disease. The church accepts that everyone has the right to defend one's life against mortal danger. This would include using the appropriate means and course of action.

Similarly, where one spouse is infected with HIV/AIDS they must listen to their consciences. They are the only ones who can choose the appropriate means in order to defend themselves against the infection. Decisions of such an intimate nature should be made by both husband and wife as equal and loving partners.

Heed Christ's Words

We proclaim Christ's message to you, the people of today, "The kingdom of God is near. Turn away from your sin, and believe in the good news" (Mk. 1:15).

So often we blame God or other people for what happens to us. Instead we have to take responsibility for our actions before God. This involves listening to God's word and to the teaching of the church so that we can have informed and mature consciences.

The message of the Gospel is very different from that which we receive from television, videos, Internet, newspapers and magazines, which so often promote uncontrolled sex and infidelity.

Dear people of God. We have to solve our problems in this "kingdom way." Therefore let us heed the call of Christ to return to the way of self-control and fidelity. St. Paul encourages us to shine among corrupt people like stars lighting up the sky as we offer them the message of life (see Phil. 2:15–16).

Call to Action

We call on all people of our nations to break the silence around HIV/AIDS by calling AIDS, AIDS and by accepting people who are living with this disease.

We express our deep appreciation to all who are working generously (and very often with little remuneration) for people living with AIDS and for AIDS orphans.

We also pay tribute to the priests, religious sisters and brothers and to men and women of the community who so often work quietly and generously to bring Christ's healing ministry to the most neglected and forgotten.

As bishops we are proud of the enormous outreach in every diocese in AIDS prevention, caring for those living with AIDS and those affected by AIDS, especially children and orphans.

We call on small Christian communities, prayer groups, sodalities, priests, religious and pastoral workers to join hands with all people who are engaged in the struggle against AIDS.

We wish also to encourage others to volunteer their time to visit and care for those who are afflicted by this disease.

AIDS must never be considered as a punishment from God. He wants us to be healthy and not to die from AIDS. It is for us a sign of the times, challenging all people to inner transformation and to the following of Christ in his ministry of healing, mercy and love.

Call to Prayer

We invite all people to unite in prayer to Almighty God in this time of crisis in our nations. In the past in South Africa we approached God to help us in our struggle for freedom and human dignity, and we experienced the great miracle of transition. Now we pray for another "miracle" to bring us that inner freedom which will enable our nations to choose the right way to uphold human dignity in our new struggle—the battle against HIV/AIDS. Jesus is with us still today on our way of the cross of HIV/AIDS.

Jesus invites us in his hour of agony to join him in deep prayer to the Father as the way to resurrection and life.

May the Lord guide us all, give us strength and touch us with his healing hand.

> "If the present level of government inaction
> continues, it is likely that 50 million
> Africans will die before there is an effective
> vaccine."

African Governments Should Take Steps to Combat AIDS

John C. Caldwell

In the following viewpoint John C. Caldwell asserts that African governments must end their unwillingness to respond to the AIDS crisis. According to Caldwell, African heads of state have done little to reduce the spread of AIDS because they fear alienating their citizens, who disapprove of many AIDS-fighting responses because of conservative beliefs about sexuality, and contradicting the views of conservative religious leaders. Caldwell maintains that African governments need to move past these concerns and recognize the social and sexual reality of their citizens. Among the actions Caldwell believes governments should take are offering educational programs, encouraging the use of condoms, and increasing the availability of sexually transmitted disease treatments. Caldwell is a professor emeritus of demography at the Australian National University in Canberra.

As you read, consider the following questions:

1. According to Caldwell, what proportion of Nigerian Christian leaders believe AIDS is divine punishment?
2. In the author's opinion, how did African governments misinterpret the failure of education to end the AIDS epidemic?

John C. Caldwell, "Rethinking the African AIDS Epidemic," *Population and Development Review*, vol. 26, March 2000. Reproduced by permission of Population Council.

The reasons given to explain how a major heterosexually driven AIDS epidemic came about in sub-Saharan Africa are insufficient to explain why it has persisted. . . . There has in fact been no change recorded at the national level except in Uganda, where HIV infection rates appear to have fallen among the population under 25 years of age. This lack of change has for some years now been the focus of our program; our conclusion is that this situation should not have been allowed to persist and is reversible. It is not an insoluble African problem. . . .

[A 1992 article by John C. Caldwell, I.O. Orubuloye, and Pat Caldwell] noted that no one blamed governments for inaction. Nowhere had there been riots or even demonstrations, and this is still the case even in countries where over one-quarter of adults are seropositive and where most of the deaths are from AIDS. This is one of the reasons why governments are not disposed to take effective action. They fear creating for themselves more trouble than the AIDS epidemic already causes them. Heads of state do not wish to be associated with the epidemic, and, in spite of much protest from the Lusaka conference,[1] not a single president or prime minister attended it, even for the opening and closing ceremonies. The other reason for inaction is that many politicians regard the disease largely as their electorate does. Much of the action that has been taken has been by foreign-funded nongovernmental organizations (NGOs) or as part of programs partly planned and largely funded by international donors.

Views on Sexuality

The problems that African governments have in communicating with their citizens, with outsiders, and among themselves were exposed at the Lusaka meeting. After 20 years of the AIDS epidemic, policy discussions are still full of abstract planning language, with promises to organize, decentralize, and base the work within the community. There was no desire among government representatives to discuss pre-

1. referring to the 11th International Conference on AIDS and STDs in Africa, held in September 1999 in Lusaka, Zambia

cisely what would work in the local setting and why. This was jarringly different from the down-to-earth language and examples offered at family planning conferences and immunization workshops. There is a fear of alienating their followers by intruding into sexual matters and by speaking aloud on such subjects. There is a fear of failure. Above all there is a fear of confronting those who regard the only solution to be confining sexual activity within marriage, either because it is the law of God or because it will Westernize the family and modernize society. Three-quarters of Christian leaders in Nigeria believe that AIDS is a divine punishment, and the proportion is unlikely to be lower in East and Southern Africa or among the laity of the congregations. The Catholic Church holds that the use—and hence the distribution—of condoms is forbidden. Most adults regard it as immoral to provide adolescents with condoms and are reluctant to admit that the great majority are sexually active: either these views are held by the politicians themselves or else the leaders are daunted by those who do hold them. Even though AIDS has already killed well over 10 million Africans and at least 20 million more are moving toward death, there is little political gain to be had by helping to stop those numbers from multiplying.

On the other hand, we now know things that were not clear a decade ago. The first is that the unrestricted continuation of the epidemic is not a failure of the AIDS educational effort. The Demographic and Health Survey program has shown that among men 98 percent knew of AIDS in 1991–92 in Tanzania, 99 percent in 1992 in Zambia and in 1998 in Kenya. For women at those dates the proportions were 93 percent in Tanzania and 99 percent in Zambia and Kenya. A more anthropological approach can show an inadequate knowledge of some methods of transmission or of the nature of the pathogen, but almost all Africans know that there is a sinister new disease, AIDS, that it is sexually transmitted, that it is more likely to be caught if one has multiple partners or participates in commercial sex, and that the disease kills most people it infects. A decade ago it was believed that such knowledge should be sufficient to contain the epidemic. In this sense the educational approach has failed, although massive education will still be needed, partly to show that the message has not been reconsidered and partly because it might achieve other ends such as strengthening the fear of death.

Why Governments Are Crucial

The role of government in [addressing the AIDS epidemic] is crucial for several reasons. First, only governments can put AIDS at the centre of the national agenda—and not just on the health agenda. Second, only governments can create more favourable conditions for others to play their role. Since the 1980s civil society, non-governmental organisations (NGOs) and some religious groups have taken the lead against the epidemic. They continue to work hard in difficult circumstances. Governments can create the policy and legal environment to enable them to be more effective. Third, only governments can adequately protect the poor and those who are especially vulnerable to the HIV virus by breaking the silence, eliminating discrimination and providing adequate protection; by reducing household poverty to keep women out of the sex trade, while improving access to information, condom and STD care.

Nana K. Poku, *Third World Quarterly*, April 2001.

We also know that the tide can probably be turned against the epidemic by the same means—or at least variations of them—used to contain it elsewhere. Two international firms in the Ivory Coast have provided their workers and their families with good health services and have made condoms readily available to any individuals in these families. STD [sexually transmitted disease] levels and apparently HIV incidence have fallen as steeply as in Thailand. The same approach has been taken in the villages of the Niger River Delta in Nigeria from which the oil companies draw their workers, with the result that STD prevalence fell by 40 percent in one year. . . .

The Need for Strong Leadership

We postulate that seroprevalence would now be falling rather than rising in East and Southern Africa if governments provided strong positive leadership in identifying the AIDS epidemic as needing the government involvement and social mobilization typical of a state of total war (the mortality figures are similar to those one would expect from prolonged armed conflict); in exerting effective pressure to raise the level of condom use in completely commercial sexual relationships to 90 or 95 percent; and in ensuring that sexually active adolescents have easy access to condoms and are encouraged to use them. . . .

Lowering the Infection Rate

The African AIDS epidemic can be defeated by means already known and easily implemented. Its defeat should be an international priority justifying international pressure on, and inducements offered to, the African governments involved. At the end of 1997 almost 10 million sub-Saharan Africans had died of AIDS and another 20 million were infected and waiting to die. If the present level of government inaction continues, it is likely that 50 million Africans will die before there is an effective vaccine, and numbers could go much higher still.

To begin to contain the epidemic will not necessitate stopping all HIV transmission. What is necessary, as with all epidemics, is to ensure that the average number of people infected by each person already infected falls below one, preferably well below one. This can be achieved by reducing transmission where it is at the highest levels, through ensuring both that a very high proportion of strictly commercial sexual relations are accompanied by the use of condoms and that a high proportion of premarital adolescent sexual activity involves the use of condoms. Both would require much highly motivated activity by national governments. These activities would be most likely to succeed if they were accompanied by (1) a continuing education program focusing as now on the danger of HIV infection, but stressing more the necessity of using condoms and the horror of unnecessary death; (2) an efficient system for distributing condoms by different routes, some allowing the recipients to preserve their anonymity; and (3) a much greater provision for STD treatment so as to reduce the role of cofactors in HIV transmission.

Governments have not moved to a kind of wartime footing in order to carry out these steps for a number of reasons. First, there is a lack of reality in the society and in governments about the enormous scale of deaths and impending deaths. Second, there is an astonishing reluctance by governments and many church leaders to recognize the African sexual system. This was the case a decade ago among many African academics, researchers, and intellectuals when we published "The Social Context of AIDS in Sub-Saharan Africa" and "The Family and Sexual Networking in Sub-Saharan Africa," but most seem to have changed their views. In contrast, governments and some outside agencies misinterpret the failure of the educational effort to curb the epidemic as a sign that the effort was not good enough or was not understood, rather than that it met with deliberate resistance from people satisfied with their sexual system and unprepared to change. Third, there is still no real recognition by governments or many religious leaders of the rights of civil society, in which people deserve help in avoiding death even if their sexual behavior is at odds with the preached orthodoxy.

This summary captures the essence of the situation, and is the one on which action should be based, but it still needs some modification. The first point is that there has apparently been a decline in HIV levels in one African country, Uganda, and note should be taken of its experience. As yet the evidence for that decline comes from a very small number of urban antenatal clinics, and no evaluation has been published of possible changes in the composition of the clients. A recent analysis of the situation concluded that behavioral change must be occurring, but only because this was the residual category after other changes had been excluded. Assuming that a decline in seroprevalence has taken place, the reason is almost certainly the strong leadership of President Yoweri Museveni since 1986 and his insistence that AIDS should be discussed and identified as a national crisis needing action. On the other hand, there is little evidence of unusually high levels of condom use among adolescents or in commercial sex. Uganda was one of the first two or three countries in sub-Saharan Africa to suffer from a major AIDS epidemic, and effective behavioral change took another dozen years to occur. The longer experience of AIDS deaths may have had an impact, and AIDS mortality, selective in terms of high-risk sexual behavior, may also have played a role. Before the change came, Uganda had lost almost 10 percent of its population to AIDS deaths, with another 5 percent currently infected, probably the world's greatest losses and together similar to the Soviet Union's proportional losses in World War II. This is not, then, such a success story as suggested by those placing all their hopes on behavioral change.

The second point is that there is not the homogeneity of risk that is found among homosexual partners in the West. Most women do not lead sex lives as fraught with risk as those of their husbands. Probably about half of those with the disease were infected by their husbands. Therefore, they need support in persuading their husbands to lead less risky sex lives. They also need to be able to reject husbands suspected of high-risk sexual behavior. But their even more immediate need is to reduce the likelihood of their husbands being infected, utilizing all the means suggested here.

Recognizing Reality

The central plank in the victory over AIDS is the recognition by African governments of social and sexual reality. Millions of people are being allowed to die on the grounds that the only way they can be saved is by adopting a more "moral" way of life, indeed a way of life that does not conform to their morality. An unreal view of society still stalks African regional AIDS meetings.

Working within a framework of reality will be difficult. In the case of sexually active adolescents, if they are to recognize themselves as a sexual community with special needs in the way Australia's gay community did, then they will have to be induced to provide their own organizations and leadership (in East and Southern Africa age grade organizations may provide a basis). Such organizations may prove to be the best way of channeling condoms to them. Something similar may be part of the solution in the case of prostitutes, except that the government will have to exert its strength to protect them by forcing the cooperation of landlords, bar and hotel owners, and ultimately their clients. The vigor will have to come from the heads of state and their more powerful ministers, and the encouragement may have to come from donors. At present, reality is slipping away, as the Lusaka Conference demonstrated, toward placing hope in millions of villagers successfully living on courses of antiretroviral medications or turning to indigenous herbal medicine. Finally, strong informational programs must continue to point out the reduction in the risk of AIDS from changed sexual behavior, but this should not be presented as the only option and vigorous efforts will be needed to make the other options as risk-free as possible.

"The fight against AIDS in Africa has been dominated by long-standing Western prejudices."

The International Response to AIDS in Africa Is a Racist Failure

Alison Katz

The international health community's response to Africa's AIDS crisis has failed because it is based on racist notions, Alison Katz asserts in the following viewpoint. According to Katz, Western organizations such as the World Bank and the United Nation's AIDS programs operate on the assumption that African promiscuity is the primary cause of AIDS while ignoring the connections between poverty and disease. She asserts that the international community could better serve Africans by eradicating poverty and providing the basic necessities, such as food and sanitation, to ensure good health for all Africans. Katz is a member of the People's Health Movement, an organization that aims to make health care a priority in local, national, and international policy making.

As you read, consider the following questions:

1. What percentage of adults in Botswana is HIV-positive?
2. According to the author, what are some of the biological factors that have led to the high rate of HIV in impoverished populations?
3. In Katz's view, what is the responsibility of international health authorities?

"Thirteen million AIDS deaths already in the worst affected countries. Without care and treatment, there will be 68 million more between now and 2020." The global figures on AIDS are terrifying, but the first reaction of a number of world experts (of other diseases) to the above announcement at the International AIDS Conference in Barcelona, July 2002, was indignation. They protested that Peter Piot, executive director of UNAIDS [United Nations Programme on AIDS], must be stealing some of his figures from "their diseases." Such is politics in the international health community.

Politics on a grander scale has prevented a rational and effective response to the AIDS pandemic, which is killing up to a quarter of many southern African countries' populations. The real scandal is not the unseemly scrambling after donor funds, but the imperceptible impact of international and national responses to AIDS over two decades of intense and costly activity. In its sobering 2002 report, UNAIDS states that prevalence is climbing higher than ever previously believed possible. It is spreading rapidly into new populations in Africa, Asia, the Caribbean, and Eastern Europe.

One third of Zimbabwe's population is infected and the epidemic continues to expand even in countries that already had extremely high HIV prevalence. In Botswana for example, the country with the highest HIV infection rates in the world, almost 39 percent of all adults are now living with HIV, up from less than 36 percent 2 years ago.

Are we doing something wrong? Is the approach ill founded or even fatally flawed? Neither UNAIDS nor any of its partners are even asking the question let alone revising their strategies.

A Neo-Liberal Approach

For over 20 years now, the international AIDS community has persisted in a reductionist obsession with individual behavior and an implicit acceptance of a deeply flawed and essentially racist theory.

In line with neo-liberal doctrine, it has explained the spread of AIDS—and the extremely high prevalences in sub-Saharan Africa—in terms of individual sexual behavior. It has exaggerated the extent to which people control their lives and circumstances and ignored larger macroeconomic and political factors and poverty-induced population vulnerability in terms of seriously weakened immune systems. The insistence on analyzing this colossal public health catastrophe in terms of individual behavior has correspondingly restricted the response to action at the individual level, usually promotion of safer sex, condom use, and education for prevention.

Predictably, the impact of these peripheral efforts has been insignificant, although tired old success stories are still regularly wheeled out for display. As long as the root causes of AIDS continue to be neglected, such efforts will remain cosmetic, unsustainable, and exceptions. Average HIV prevalences in the adult population of most sub-Saharan African countries are 25 percent. The figures for Europe and most of the industrialized world are still under 0.1 percent and in many cases, under 0.01 percent. Individual behavior cannot possibly account for this enormous difference, which would imply that people in some African countries have at least 250 and even 2,500 times more unprotected/unsafe sex than people in Europe, the U.S., or Australia.

The absurdity of this proposition, which has its origins in racist mythology, is not confronted because assumptions about sexual behavior are usually implicit. Myths thrive precisely because they are unstated and therefore rarely subjected to scrutiny. Running parallel to this dubious proposition is the perverse refusal to confront the obvious, such as the almost perfect "coincidence" of high prevalence of HIV/AIDS (and all the diseases of poverty) with the poorest regions of the earth.

An epidemic of gigantic proportions is taking hold in Southeast Asia, home to an even larger number of powerless and poverty stricken people. It will be interesting to see if any notion of structural violence is at last invoked to advance our understanding of the dynamics of the pandemic or if we will discover that previously quite "well-behaved" Asians are as "promiscuous" as Africans.

The fundamental public health lessons of the past 150 years are known even to lay people. It is well understood that the overall health status of populations and their capacity to fight off infection is related primarily to food, water, sanitation, and housing. According to an article by [Eileen] Stillwaggon, "HIV/AIDS in Africa: Fertile Terrain," published in the *Journal of Development Studies* (August 2002): "A century of clinical practice demonstrates that people with nutritional deficiencies, parasitic diseases, generally poor health and little access to health services or who are otherwise economically disadvantaged have greater susceptibility to infectious diseases whether they are transmitted sexually, by food, water, air or other means."

An Imperialist Epidemic

Evidence shows that the HIV virus is the infectious agent that causes the spread from individual to individual. But the existence of a worldwide *epidemic*—especially in the African continent—of HIV infection and AIDS is fundamentally caused by social conditions, including poverty, drug addiction, reactionary religious views and practices, male supremacy and associated sexual practices, national oppression, and the deliberate indifference of capitalist medical establishments to a disease concentrated among the poor.

In short, the disease is spread via a virus, but the *epidemic* is caused by the system—by class society, its reactionary social relations, and the poverty of the people. The conditions under which the AIDS epidemic has spread in the African continent are tied, by a thousand threads, to imperialism, neo-colonialism, and apartheid.

Revolutionary Worker, August 6, 2000.

Curiously, in the case of HIV/AIDS, seriously deficient immune systems have been ignored as a factor of vulnerability and determinant of the high levels of infection in desperately poor populations.

[Scientist Louis] Pasteur's dictum, "the microbe is nothing, the terrain is everything," is still the best summary of century-old public health wisdom. The focus on individual behavior is almost as absurd in the response to AIDS as it would be if it were applied to the response to tuberculosis. A sound public health approach to TB does not exhort people in high prevalence areas not to breathe too much on each other—not understanding that they are breathing more or less like every other human being on earth. It addresses the sanitary, nutritional, and housing arrangements, which determine their high vulnerability.

Breathing and having sex—though not quite in the same category—can both reasonably be seen as everyday human behaviors. The peculiar focus on the exotic, the unusual, the immoral, and the illegal has obscured the simple fact that AIDS is overwhelmingly transmitted through heterosexual, penetrative, vaginal sex. Few people know that when AIDS hit the headlines as a "gay plague" in California it was already a well established heterosexual epidemic in Africa. The unimportance, in the eyes of the world, of African people in general, and of African women in particular, may partly explain this neglect. The common sense interpretation of the facts is that high risk physical and economic environments, coupled with dangerously weakened immune systems, leave people highly susceptible to all kinds of infections including HIV.

Race and Gender

The fight against AIDS in Africa has been dominated by long-standing Western prejudices against African sexuality and cultural practices. A striking example was in the early 1980s, when speculation about the Haitian origin of AIDS and the role of bizarre voodoo practices led to a wave of anti-Haitian discrimination. As with Jamaica, the Dominican Republic, and Trinidad, it turned out that tourists (mainly U.S. homosexuals) were the most likely source of virus transmission. It has been pointed out that in the absence of penicillin, the war-ravaged Europe of the late 1940s would have been devastated by epidemics of syphilis and gonorrhea.

The international AIDS community has pursued a singularly unsuccessful strategy with religious conviction, rather than with good science or even common sense. Evidence, in the rather odious academic area known euphemistically as "sexual networking," is flimsy. Rates of sexual activity do not appear to vary much between populations (though of course there are always groups within populations who either take more risks or have more risks imposed on them). What seems to emerge from the literature with consistency is that multiple, mostly serial, casual, and unprotected sex is common in Africa, Europe, the U.S., and parts of Asia, with most men everywhere having more partners than most women.

Furthermore, rates/types of sexual activity do not appear to have a clear relation with prevalence of HIV infection. A major multi-site study undertaken by UNAIDS in four sub-Saharan African cities showed that most parameters of risky sexual behavior were not consistently more common in the high HIV prevalence sites than in the relatively low prevalence sites.

The implicit assumption that African people have more or less "brought it on themselves" through their "promiscuity" has evolved through a superficial, neo-liberal gender analysis into a much more explicit accusation of African men. If such an apolitical gender debate has resulted in shifting the blame from all African people to all African men, it has failed. No one disputes that women, particularly in developing countries, are not only biologically more vulnerable to sexually transmitted infections including HIV, but they are also acutely vulnerable socially, culturally and economically. Women have to exchange sex for material favors for their own and their children's survival in many poor countries. For as long as they do not control when, where, with whom, with or without protection, they have sex—they will be at risk.

However, women in Europe are clearly at far less risk than men in Africa. If we take as a rough indicator of risk, the average prevalences of less than 0.1 percent and 25 percent for Europe and Africa respectively, it becomes clear that neither individual behavior nor gender inequality accounts for the spread and pattern of the pandemic. Sound feminist analysis, rooted in social justice, recognizes oppression of women in poor countries within the context of the oppression of entire communities of men, women, and children, none of whom have any meaningful control over their lives.

Women in sub-Saharan Africa carry a risk of contracting HIV infection at a rate 500–1,000-fold compared to women in the rest of the world. This is quite a large difference to explain in terms of African and European male sexual behavior.

A Disease of Poverty

In common with all sexually transmitted infections (STIs), HIV/AIDS has a particular relationship to poverty. The poor are more vulnerable to HIV infection than the rich—notwithstanding transient vulnerabilities of richer men who can afford to use prostitutes—of which much has been made. The fact remains that 95 percent of infections are in developing countries; and more than 70 percent are in sub-Saharan Africa where over 80 percent of the deaths have occurred. Women are more vulnerable than men; young women are far more vulnerable (4 to 5 times) than young men. Oppressed and marginalized "minorities"—blacks and Hispanics in the U.S., refugees and street children everywhere—are more vulnerable than dominant majorities.

There are plausible explanations, in terms of biological vulnerability, for the very high rates of HIV transmission among poor populations. The major biological factors of interest are malnutrition and chronic co-infection with other diseases of poverty, notably, parasitic infection, tuberculosis, malaria, and other tropical diseases. These factors are known to seriously impair and interfere with immune function, and to be responsible for the bulk of infectious disease—whether bacterial, viral, or parasitic.

The thesis that is proposed for the huge variation in prevalence between countries is that HIV-negative people whose immune systems are weakened by poor nutrition and constantly challenged by co-infections are more vulnerable to HIV infection; and that HIV-positive people, in the same condition, are more infectious to others. The result is high population transmission rates.

There is no shortage of evidence on the adverse, even devastating effects of malnutrition, under-nutrition, and specific nutritional deficiencies on immune function, susceptibility to infection and capacity to cope, once infected.

The term nutritionally acquired immune deficiency syndrome (NAIDS) is applied to immunological dysfunction associated with malnutrition in infants and small children. Is it unreasonable to suppose that a similar mechanism may operate in adolescents and adults and may be worth investigating and even—as a precautionary principle—acting on? The average African household is caught in a poverty cycle of low food production, low income, poor health, malnutrition, poor environmental sanitation, and infectious disease. Food security, as primary prevention, should be a priority strategy in the fight against AIDS in Africa. With water and sanitation, it has the huge advantage of simultaneously reducing population vulnerability to all the other diseases of poverty.

The Effects of Co-Infections

This brings us to the second major factor, chronic co-infections, most of which are also related to the failure to meet basic needs. There is ample evidence that co-infections not only interfere with immune function, but they also increase viremia—the level of HIV circulating in the body. High viremea, unsurprisingly, is associated with increased risk of transmission.

Parasitic infections, which affect over a quarter of the world's population, overwhelmingly in developing countries, may play a particularly important role in high population transmission rates of HIV and TB. Some researchers have suggested that in order to control both these epidemics, parasitic infections must be controlled first. The only co-infection that has received due attention is sexually transmitted infection (syphilis, gonorrhea, chancroid etc), which is known to substantially increase vulnerability to HIV infection. Prevention and control of STI has been recognized as a key strategy in the fight against AIDS.

Interestingly, the fact that the modes of transmission are the same for STIs as for HIV—both are blood borne diseases, which can be transmitted sexually—has meant that the focus on individual behavior and individual agency can go unchallenged. This would not be the case if the co-infection to be prevented or controlled as a factor of susceptibility to HIV infection were intestinal worms or enteritis.

With the exception of some brave and outspoken NGOs [nongovernmental organizations], the mainstream international AIDS community steadfastly refuses to address poverty, powerlessness, and inequality. It is not that the AIDS community does not talk about poverty. On the contrary, it is the most fashionable subject at the moment. Poverty reduction (rather than eradication) is on everyone's lips in the alliance of WB/IMF/WTO/G8,[1] the UN agencies dealing with AIDS, government aid agencies, and "charitable" foundations, such as Ford, Rockefeller, and Bill and Melinda Gates.

In sanctimonious tones, they lament the persistence of poverty, but in a perverse reversal of logic, they advocate for massive attacks on a few killer diseases (malaria, TB, and AIDS) in order to "create prosperity." No amount of health delivered to Haitians or Tanzanians today is going to provide them with prosperity tomorrow or the next day. It will allow them to survive where others die in rather precarious conditions, perhaps until the next bout of illness.

Many will protest that the connections with poverty have been recognized from the start. This is true, but it has invariably been in terms of the economic impact of AIDS on communities, in particular on their productivity rather than poverty as the root cause of extreme susceptibility to all infections including HIV.

Behavior-Centered Solutions

Even when social and economic factors, such as labor migration, exchange of sex for survival, gender power imbalances and population movements, have been identified as contributing to vulnerability, the solutions proposed are still focused on the residual action possible at the level of individual behavior.

The most striking example of this is the provision of condoms at the pithead of mines in South Africa to tens of thousands of migrant laborers slaving to bring up gold for white-owned transnational corporations and to thousands of migrant women selling sex to feed and clothe their children. Migrant labor and sex slavery are unhealthy—even life threatening—socially constructed phenomena, which can therefore be socially deconstructed. Examination of poverty and powerlessness as root causes of AIDS would threaten these kinds of production arrangements. They would also imply a fundamental shift in the international economic or-

1. respectively, the World Bank, International Monetary Fund, World Trade Organization, and the collection of eight industrialized nations that make up the G8

der, massive redistribution of the earth's resources, and an end to the fantastically exploitative relations between North and South.

The overwhelming power of vested interests confines both the research agenda and the strategies of the international AIDS community to the sphere of the individual in order that structural, economic, and political inequalities neither be brought to light nor questioned.

The Declaration of Alma Ata (International Conference on Primary Health Care) in 1978 explicitly recognized structural inequalities and macroeconomic factors as determinants of poverty and therefore of population health status. As this approach threatened the status quo, it was politically sanitized and reduced to a few technological interventions. By the early 1980s, neo-liberal dogma was already being imposed in international fora and primary health care had more or less been abandoned.

However, the only progress possible in public health today, and in the fight against AIDS, is a return to the wisdom of Alma Ata—armed at the turn of the century with 20 years' more evidence of the negative health effects of savage, free market neo-liberalism. The "triumph" of capitalism in the Russian Federation, for example, has been accompanied by the collapse of health services and spectacular increases in rates of illness and death.

The Responsibility of the International Community

The sums made available through international aid are pitiful compared to the sums that would be released through debt cancellation, fair trade, and measures to end the continued pillage of developing country resources. These amount to trillions rather than millions. It is not hard to understand the preference for international aid. First, it brings about one and a half times more back to the donor country than is received by the recipient country. Second, it is immediately used to service the debt to Northern banks—far larger sums than are available to the health and education sectors of debtor countries. Third, even though it may increase the size of the crumbs from the rich person's table, it does not threaten the international economic order. On the contrary, it deepens the dependency that is so profitable to the developed countries and so devastating to developing countries.

It is the responsibility of international health authorities to identify the determinants of health (and disease) and to advocate for policy and action, which will contribute most effectively to the goal of health for all, even if this lies outside the health sector. If food, water, sanitation, basic health care, and housing are the quickest, cheapest, most effective ways of achieving health for all, then the international health community should be advocating this.

If these basic needs can only be met when countries' national capacities are freed from the strangulation of debt and unfair terms of trade and from the destabilizing chaos of financial flows then they must recommend this. If national food security requires a degree of protectionism rather than unfettered free trade, it must be strongly advocated. There could be no clearer public health imperative. If the obstacle to such advocacy is the hand that feeds the international AIDS community, then the time has come to bite it. That hand is the alliance of WB/IMF/WTO, the G8—even occasionally the UN—and the transnational corporations influencing their policies.

The beauty of a fair international economic order lies in the fact that nations, communities, and families left to their own devices are quite capable of meeting their own basic needs. Removing the obstacles to self-determination is the task to be accomplished.

The international AIDS community needs to ally with the tremendous movement for social and economic justice today. As a start it might wish to make immediate debt cancellation . . . followed swiftly by the first steps towards fair trade, bringing trillions of dollars to public health efforts within the long promised new international economic order.

"The U.S. churches are in a unique position to lend support to African efforts to combat [AIDS]."

American Churches Should Take a Larger Role in Reducing the Spread of AIDS in Africa

Eugene F. Rivers III and Jacqueline C. Rivers

American churches should form partnerships with each other and with African churches to address AIDS in Africa, Eugene F. Rivers III and Jacqueline C. Rivers contend in the following viewpoint. The authors opine that U.S. church leaders can reduce the spread of the disease by educating Africans on the ways poverty and sexual behavior affect AIDS, lobbying international lending agencies and pharmaceutical companies, and providing humanitarian assistance to AIDS orphans and people dying from the disease. Eugene F. Rivers III is a pastor and a contributing editor to *Sojourners.* He and Jacqueline C. Rivers are the cochairs of the National Ten-Point Leadership Foundation, a coalition that organizes partnerships between clergy, law enforcement, and the community in order to help end violence among inner-city youth.

As you read, consider the following questions:

1. How much money did South Africa spend on AIDS programs between 1995 and 2000, according to the authors?
2. With which organizations should black churches form an alliance, in the authors' view?
3. According to the Rivers, what is the primary question that must be addressed by the church?

Eugene F. Rivers III and Jacqueline C. Rivers, "The Fight for the Living," *Sojourners*, vol. 29, July/August 2000, pp. 18, 20–22. Copyright © 2000 by *Sojourners*. (800) 714-7474, www.sojo.net. Reproduced by permission.

Throughout human history, tragedies have served as opportunities for the church to be a source of hope, conscience, and witness. In the crucible of unbelievable human suffering, God offers various generations the privilege to be a light during seasons of great moral tragedy.

Fortunately, such occasions of world historical significance are rare. On such occasions, the church has too frequently failed to obey God's call to be a witness against despair and death, and then stands naked before God and the world with the blood of the innocent on its hands. The church's inadequate response to the destruction of European Jewry during World War II and the genocide in Rwanda are clear and unfortunate examples of such missed opportunities.

Admittedly, such crises are complex and do not yield to simplistic rhetoric or solutions. And on more than a few questions, well-intentioned solutions are worse than the "disease" they are intended to cure. However, even with the complexities and tragedy noted, the church is obligated to stand on the side of the poor and neglected.

An Immense Crisis

At the beginning of [the twenty-first] century, the church in the United States has a unique challenge and opportunity to be a powerful voice of conscience and practical reason in the face of the greatest humanitarian crisis of our times: The AIDS holocaust in sub-Saharan Africa.

AIDS is the leading cause of death in sub-Saharan Africa. Consider the facts:

- Of the 5.6 million new HIV infections in 1999, according to the U.N. Program on AIDS, fully 4 million were in Africa. Half were among young people ages 15 to 24, and far more than half of those afflicted were female.

- Two-thirds of the AIDS cases in the world are now in sub-Saharan Africa. One adult in four in Namibia, Zimbabwe, Swaziland, and Botswana now has the HIV virus. Half of these cases in sub-Saharan Africa are women.

- The numbers are so massive in southern Africa that life expectancy is likely to drop to 45 years within the next five years after climbing to 59 in the early 1990s. [Since 1995]— according to a U.S. Census Bureau report—life expectancy in Zimbabwe has dropped from 61 years to 39 years; in Botswana it has fallen from 60 to 40, and in Kenya the situation is very similar.

As unbelievable as these statistics are, things are only getting worse. A survey of prenatal clinics in one southern province in Zimbabwe indicated a 67 percent infection rate for the women there. In Zambia there are communities consisting of only the elderly and the very young; the rest have been obliterated. The AIDS epidemic is even contributing to the deforestation of significant areas—because of coffin construction. In southern Africa we are witnessing the creation of a virtual biological underclass.

Troubling Conduct

In this situation in which millions are perishing, the behavior of the citizens of the affected countries is profoundly troubling. For example, it is reported that in South Africa a woman is raped every 26 seconds, contributing to the 1,600 people a day who are infected with HIV. Just as disturbing is the rumored source of the increase in the rate of rape: a spreading myth that sexual intercourse with young girls can cure or prevent the disease.

Behind the statistics on rape lurk facts that are in some respects just as ominous. In sub-Saharan Africa, AIDS is transmitted primarily through heterosexual contact. Widespread promiscuity—essentially fatal behavior—is typical. The head of the UNAIDS [United Nations Programme on AIDS] program for Eastern and Southern Africa said, "without addressing behavior, the response to prevention strategies will always be limited." Promiscuity and rape now objectively function as weapons of suicidal mass destruction. In such a context of cultural decay, abstinence and sexual fidelity appear as revolutionary concepts.

Within five years, 61 of every 1,000 children born in Namibia, Botswana, Zimbabwe, Swaziland, and South Africa won't reach their first birthday, according to U.N. estimates. By 2001 there will be 13 million AIDS orphans in sub-Saharan Africa, according to figures presented at the September 1999 International AIDS conference in Zambia.

In too many cases African leaders have not confronted the

problem of AIDS: The South African government has spent only $13 million on AIDS education and care programs [since 1995]. At the same time it is spending $6.5 *billion* on three new submarines and other military hardware. Not a single African head of state attended the AIDS conference in Zambia, including the president of the host country. Unfortunately this is not an isolated incident, but an example of a pattern of deliberate neglect by these leaders.

While these African nations obviously do *not* have the resources to treat AIDS victims using the extremely expensive cocktail of drugs now widely available in the West, their public education efforts have clearly failed to communicate to the masses of citizens the urgency of the situation and the exigencies of preventative behavior. Deep-rooted cultural patterns are implicated, which call for sensitively crafted solutions. It does not appear that many African governments have engaged the issues at this level.

Three Main Tasks

In order to address the crisis, black and white churches in the United States, both Protestant and Catholic, must work in strategic partnerships to address both the long-term and the short-term foreign and development policy implications of the AIDS crisis in Africa.

In view of the horror that confronts literally millions of African women and children, U.S. church leaders face three main tasks: public education, political advocacy, and humanitarian assistance.

Education. U.S. church leaders have the political clout and the access to the levers of power that are needed to educate elected officials about this issue. At the same time the public, especially the black public, must be educated to advocate for foreign and development policy decisions that will support and encourage African governments in their efforts to confront this crisis. Black Protestant and Catholic students, seminarians, and intellectuals must now mount a grassroots campaign that focuses on the relationship among sexual behaviors, AIDS, and poverty.

Political advocacy. The churches must challenge African leadership to be more accountable to the needs of their own women and children. We must, on humanitarian grounds, challenge African leaders to mobilize their societies to exact a high price for rape.

This raises an important question: Why haven't black churches, especially the seven major black denominations, used their unique position to serve as more effective advocates for the needs and interests of millions of orphans in Africa? They should develop a strategic alliance with the IMF [International Monetary Fund], the World Bank, and other international lending agencies to demand debt cancellation for African nations, thereby freeing up financial resources to be redirected towards the AIDS crisis.

HIV/AIDS Infection Rate Among Adults in Some Sub-Saharan African Countries

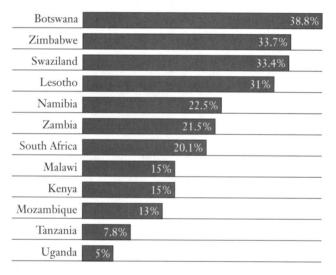

Country	Rate
Botswana	38.8%
Zimbabwe	33.7%
Swaziland	33.4%
Lesotho	31%
Namibia	22.5%
Zambia	21.5%
South Africa	20.1%
Malawi	15%
Kenya	15%
Mozambique	13%
Tanzania	7.8%
Uganda	5%

UNAIDS, 2003.

It is also critical that churches apply moral, economic, and political pressure to pharmaceutical companies directly. Western pharmaceutical companies have been implicated in monopoly pricing practices, effectively shutting out access for poor Africans to life-preserving AIDS drugs. These pharmaceutical companies no longer can be permitted to exploit the suffering of millions of black people.

Humanitarian assistance. The U.S. churches are in a unique position to lend support to African efforts to combat the disease. Protestant and Catholic churches should partner with African governments to spearhead a drive to build combination boarding schools and orphanages for the 40 million children left without guardians. (In comparison, there are currently about 40 million children in the whole U.S. public school system.) With 500 children per orphanage, 80,000 such institutions must be built over the next 10 years. In addition to providing shelter, care, and education, these boarding schools–orphanages should serve as civic education and leadership development sites.

In addition to caring for orphans, these religious partnerships must focus on caring for those who are sick and dying. It is critical to break down stigmas that lead to violence against those who are sick—especially women and children. In many African countries, admitting having AIDS means ostracism, emotional and psychological abuse, and outright physical violence. Such treatment only exacerbates the fraying of community structures. It is imperative that those who are sick be treated with compassion and dignity. Religious partnerships that include African institutions and clergy can play a pivotal role in promoting community care structures. The families of the sick and dying also need support, as a further hedge against community erosion. Religious partnerships can also play a pivotal role in promoting community care structures to address these needs.

A Pan-African Response

What is needed is a pan-African, charismatic, evangelical congress working with community-based efforts to address the crisis in affected African countries. The goal of this congress would be to develop a program modeled on the Peace Corps and focused on providing assistance to the countries most ravaged by AIDS, and with the highest HIV infection rates.

The first steps towards developing this pan-African evangelical congress must be the identification of African religious entities and leaders to guide the work on the local front. Collaboration with both the private sector and the government in the United States, and with the Catholic Church here and in Africa, will be critical to the success of these efforts. Finally, a massive call to the church world and to the universities and seminaries must be issued to recruit young people with the willingness, time, and dedication to commit two years to working in such a program.

The AIDS holocaust in Africa presents the perfect political context to engage some of the most difficult policy questions in the arena of post–Cold War international relations and U.S. foreign policy. The theological and political debate must include the black, Protestant, and Catholic peace and justice communities, in strategic partnership with the academic theological community. Clergy, laity, church leaders, and theologians must deepen their understanding of the political realities of international relations and of the role of the United States, with particular focus on the implications for Africa. "The Harvest of Justice Is Sown in Peace," a 1993 statement produced by the U.S. Catholic Conference, provides useful insights into the moral dilemmas of this era.

The primary question for the church is: How does it wisely apply gospel values to define the legitimate values and interests and role of a superpower? For example, what are the necessary normative and political criteria for the construction of a coherent post–Cold War policy framework for Africa? How does the church wisely respond to international crises in which the available political actors or outcomes are less than desirable or at best morally ambiguous? Even as the church struggles to craft nuanced and convincing answers to difficult questions such as these, it must assist in the implementation of foreign policy decisions and offer oversight to others engaged in the work.

A Broad Coalition

Finally, the black church must face one vital issue of its own. New black church leadership has the responsibility to lay the groundwork for an alternative to the high visibility model of engagement in international affairs that has been practiced in some quarters, and especially the extremely low impact this model has had on policy. Black church leadership must outgrow plantation-style dependence upon the Democratic

Party. The black poor have no permanent friends, just permanent interests. Black church activists must build a broad faith coalition to promote issues relating to African development. The political leadership of both the Democratic and Republican parties must be challenged with equal vigor on the issue of AIDS and U.S. foreign policy.

Rarely has the U.S. church had a greater opportunity to speak as a fresh voice of reason and solidarity in the arena of foreign and development policy. Sub-Saharan Africa is facing a monumental tragedy in the AIDS crisis. When the history of this sexual holocaust is written, one of the most important questions to be addressed will be: What has been done by the church in the United States?

Periodical Bibliography

The following articles have been selected to supplement the diverse views presented in this chapter.

Robert Baker	"HIV Does Not Spread AIDS," *Spectator*, April 21, 2001.
Jon Cohen	"Deep Denial," *Sciences*, January 2001.
Helen Epstein and Lincoln Chen	"Can AIDS Be Stopped?" *New York Review of Books*, March 14, 2002.
Issues and Controversies On File	"Drug Patents and Developing Countries," March 28, 2003.
Musimbi Kanyoro	"The Face of AIDS," *Other Side*, May/June 2000.
Charles R. Larson	"AIDS and Africa: The End of Denial?" *World & I*, December 2000.
Joseph Loconte	"The ABCs of AIDS," *Weekly Standard*, October 27, 2003.
David Masci	"Global AIDS Crisis," *CQ Researcher*, October 13, 2000.
Mark Schoofs	"Death and the Second Sex," *Village Voice*, December 7, 1999.
Mark Schoofs	"The War *for* Drugs," *Village Voice*, March 28, 2000.
Matthew Steinglass	"It Takes a Village Healer," *Lingua Franca*, April 2001.
Emily Wax	"The ABCs of AIDS," *Washington Post National Weekly Edition*, July 14–20, 2003.
Kevin Whitelaw et al.	"In Death's Shadow," *U.S. News & World Report*, July 21, 2003.

CHAPTER 3

What Policies Will Best Help Africa?

Chapter Preface

With poverty, famine, and AIDS among its persistent problems, Africa is a continent that is often in need of international aid. However, the extent and nature of aid necessary to help Africa is a controversial topic. The solutions that were suggested on behalf of Liberia in 2003 illustrate the difficulty in finding universally accepted responses to Africa's troubles.

By 2003 Liberians had suffered through fourteen years of violence and political turmoil. On December 24, 1989, soldier Charles Taylor led troops to the capital, Monrovia, and began a guerrilla war against his former ally, President Samuel Doe. By the middle of 1990 Taylor controlled most of Liberia. In 1999, two years after Taylor won a sham election, rebel fighters took up arms against the regime. The civil war and Taylor's regime's brutality resulted in 250,000 deaths and the displacement of more than a million Liberians.

An attempt to craft a cease-fire that would end both the civil war and Taylor's reign failed in June 2003. This failure prompted Liberians to call for a peacekeeping mission by Western nations, in particular the United States. Reaction toward the situation in Liberia in America and elsewhere was mixed: Some people felt a swift military response by the United States was required while others opined that the United States should have a limited or nonexistent role in African politics.

Supporters for a military response asserted that the United States had a moral obligation to help the war-torn nation. According to the British magazine *Economist*, "Liberia's war is not only a human catastrophe; it is also destabilising much of West Africa. Liberia's president, Charles Taylor, has started or fuelled wars in three neighbouring countries: Sierra Leone, Guinea and Cote d'Ivoire. So long as he remains in power, there is a risk that the region could slide into mayhem." The magazine suggested that American troops could secure Monrovia, stabilize the nation, and then transfer responsibility to a UN force. Tom Masland, Michael Hirsh, and Tamara Lipper, writing for *Newsweek* magazine agreed: "George W. Bush likes to preach 'moral clarity' in his foreign policy. And the moral imperative in Liberia, it seems, could not be clearer: step in and stop the killing."

Other people believed the United States should not solve Liberia's problems. Former South African president F.W. de Klerk, writing an opinion piece for the *Wall Street Journal*, argued that African nations, not the United States, should send peacekeepers to Liberia. According to de Klerk, "America would find it a great deal less expensive to . . . help Africans address the problems of their continent themselves, rather than be pressured into intervening in Africa itself. It could also make Liberia a much more pleasant place to live." American foreign policy isolationists also supported the idea of staying out of Liberia, but their argument centered on the idea that the United States has no significant interest in the country and that American soldiers would not be able to quell the unrest. Srdja Trifkovic, the foreign-affairs editor of the magazine *Chronicles*, asserted, "The unpleasantness that is likely to accompany Charles Taylor's departure from power is lamentable but unavoidable. American soldiers cannot prevent or manage it; at best, they can postpone it."

President George W. Bush's administration decided on a limited military response. On August 14, 2003, more than one hundred U.S. Marines entered Liberia as part of an African-run peacekeeping force. With the peacekeepers in place, Taylor agreed to leave Liberia and begin exile in Nigeria. He handed power to his deputy, Moses Blah. The interim government, which in October 2003 named Gyude Bryant as its head, replacing Blah, signed a peace accord with the rebels. On October 1, 2003, U.S. troops departed and the peacekeeping responsibility was transferred to a UN force.

While the stability of Liberia's government will likely remain unknown until elections are held in 2005, the departure of Charles Taylor will probably improve the lives of most Liberians. As the situation in Liberia indicates, it is not an easy task for the United States and the international community to determine the best course of action in Africa. In the following chapter the authors consider which policies will best solve the numerous problems facing Africa. Whether established by Africans or by outside governments and organizations, the most effective of these solutions will help improve the quality of life on the continent.

"*The [New Partnership for Africa's Development] . . . recognizes the enormous potential creativity and dynamism of the African people.*"

The Initiatives Being Devised by Africans Will Best Improve Africa

Jean Chretien

NEPAD, or the New Partnership for Africa's Development, is an economic and political initiative devised by African governments as a way of ending poverty, bringing Africa into the global economy, and encouraging sustainable development. In the following viewpoint Canadian prime minister Jean Chretien argues that NEPAD offers hope for Africa and should be supported by industrialized nations. He notes that the goals of NEPAD have already begun to be fulfilled, as African nations move toward democracy and peace. According to Chretien, economic prosperity will follow if Canada and other industrial democracies continue to provide development assistance while also investing in and trading with Africa.

As you read, consider the following questions:
1. In Chretien's view, what factors does NEPAD acknowledge are essential in order to end Africa's economic marginalization?
2. What are some of the ties Canada has with Africa, according to the author?
3. According to Chretien, what will be the effect of a prosperous Africa?

Jean Chretien, speech to the Organization of African Unity and the United Nations Economic Commission for Africa, Addis Ababa, Ethiopia, April 11, 2002.

There is reason for hope in Africa. Canada has forgiven debt in poverty stricken countries, is investing money into Africa's development, and working with African leaders to create democratic governments, along with the G8.[1] This will bring a future of prosperity, peace, and human rights within the grasp of the African people. They have only to reach for it.

I have always believed the fundamental duty that all any government owes its people is to inspire optimism, confidence and hope; optimism about their prospects and those of their children; the confidence to follow and live their dreams; the hope, always, for a brighter tomorrow.

In saying this I am mindful of the blunt fact that Africa is a place where optimism, confidence, and hope have for too long been in short supply. Growing poverty, famine, disease, war, debt, corruption—they are the millstones of Africa. A cascade of crisis upon crisis has driven the African people to the fringes of our globalized world. I do not have to recite the statistics to you. You live them every day.

Renewing Hope

I am not known as someone of idle dreams and empty ideals. I prefer action to rhetoric. That is why I am pleased to come before you today to speak about the renewal of real hope for Africa. A renewal conceived by Africans for Africans, that puts the needs of people first. It is powered by progressive vision and values and global partnership. And, if fully implemented, will transform the relationship of Africans with each other and with the world.

I speak of course of the New Partnership for Africa's Development (NEPAD). A landmark document conceived and promoted by progressive African leaders. Rarely, if ever, has a single political initiative sought to transform an entire continent. Rarely, if ever, has such a plan been embraced so fully by the heads of government of a region, including the 53 members of the Organization of African Unity. And rarely, if ever, have we seen such commitment among leaders extend to

1. a coalition of eight major industrial democracies—United States, Canada, Japan, England, Russia, France, Germany, and Italy—who meet annually to discuss economics and politics

holding each other accountable for its full implementation.

The NEPAD is a plan of extraordinary vision, but also of immense realism. It recognizes the enormous potential creativity and dynamism of the African people. It has been shaped by their personal experience of the painful history of Africa. And it acknowledges that peace, security, democracy, good governance, human rights, and sound economic management are pre-conditions for ending the economic marginalization of the continent. It foresees a new partnership with the international community. But above all, its cornerstone is the proposition that the key to progress in Africa lies first and foremost with Africans.

Throughout Africa, we see evidence that the underlying principles of the NEPAD are taking root. For example, a lasting resolution to the endless civil war in Angola appears to be within reach. And it appears that peace between Ethiopia and Eritrea truly is being consolidated. Democracy is the birthright of all peoples, and democratic transition is becoming the norm in Africa. Moreover, tolerance for the denial of democracy is evaporating. The suspension of Zimbabwe from the Commonwealth following the report of election observers is [one] example of note.

The chairman and the convenor of the NEPAD Implementation Committee were members of the Commonwealth Troika that recommended suspension. Their decision gives proper expression to the governance principles that are integral to the NEPAD. The principles of NEPAD were not chosen at random, nor was the new concept of partnership that it envisions with the advanced industrialized countries.

Providing Effective Assistance

We will be partners in every sense of the word. It will be a two-way street, with reciprocal and integrated obligations. For our part, this includes making our development assistance more effective. And doing more to ensure that we are open to business with Africa. For your part, it means giving life to the NEPAD. African countries that are demonstrably committed to the implementation of the NEPAD in all its aspects—including good governance—will have claim to an enhanced partnership. One that promises to improve the quality of life by strengthening good government, democracy and sound economic policy; by offering support for African initiatives on education and health, agriculture and water; and by improving regional and global trade and investment. Through this new partnership we can jointly put in place the conditions that are necessary to attract resources to Africa over the long term.

Africa's Best Hope

Over the last fifty years, perhaps the greatest flaw in African development efforts is the fact that the other nations and multilateral institutions have on too many occasions imposed their models onto Africa when they were not necessarily appropriate for local practices and needs. NEPAD [New Partnership for Africa's Development] is the first comprehensive approach to African development by Africa and it deserves our serious consideration and cooperation. Whereas virtually every other large-scale plan for Africa or the developing world was conceived by international developed community and exported to Africa, NEPAD's evolution took the opposite path. It came directly from the continent itself, from four of the continent's most dynamic and committed leaders: Thabo Mbeki of South Africa, Olusegun Obasanjo of Nigeria, Abdelaziz Bouteflika of Algeria, and Abdoulaye Wade of Senegal. And now Africa is presenting its plan to the international community. As the leaders of the G8 countries did [in August 2002] in Kananaskis, Alberta, it is time to lend our support. We should dao so not because it is a perfect document. The plan is clearly not fully developed. It is an ongoing work that will require progress, and at times will certainly meet difficulties. We should support it because it represents the best of aspirations and the best hope, thus far, for Africa.

Stephen Hayes, testimony before Congress, September 18, 2002.

By demonstrating that development assistance can work we can build public support in G8 countries, which currently provide more than 70% of the development assistance available to the people of Africa. By establishing the conditions that are necessary to attract and retain private investment from Africa and abroad, we can shatter the perception all too deeply rooted that investing money in Africa doesn't pay, thereby securing capital flows that greatly exceed any foreseeable development assistance. It follows, of course, that for

Africa to truly prosper, we must open our markets to the products that such investments will generate. Only then can private capital flows have real impact in reducing poverty and increasing opportunity in Africa.

I have pledged, and I reaffirm today, that Canada will be open to business from Africa. Indeed, we recently launched consultations with Canadians on proposals for eliminating tariffs and quotas on most of the products sold to us by the least developed nations. The NEPAD is an ambitious and forward-looking proposal. It stresses the need for the engagement of the people of Africa. It reflects the lessons and mistakes of the past. It is elegant in logic and comprehensive in scope. But it cannot succeed without the will and the engagement of the industrialized world. On this point, perhaps more than ever in recent times, we have every reason to be optimistic.

Canada's Support

It will be my great honor to host the leaders of the G8 in Canada [in 2002]. As chair and with the support of G8 leaders I have made Africa a centrepiece of our agenda. Canada has long been a friend of Africa. Indeed, Canadian Jesuits founded the University of Addis Ababa. And an entire generation of Canadians was inspired by Pere Levesque who founded the University of Rwanda. And by others who personified Canada's ties with this continent. Ties nurtured through the Commonwealth and La Francophonie [French-speaking nations], and by the fact that one million Canadians are of African descent. Much of our foreign policy in recent years has been focussed on issues of special concern to Africa. Like addressing the economic causes of armed conflict such as illicit diamonds, the eradication of antipersonnel mines, ensuring the protection of civilians in armed conflict, recognizing the important role of women in society, and ending the deployment of child soldiers.

Canada has also sent peacekeepers to strife-torn regions throughout the continent. And it has demonstrated its support for Africa—and other developing countries—by taking the lead on debt. We have forgiven all the development assistance debts of almost all Heavily Indebted Poor Countries, including $1.3 billion for the 34 least developed countries in Africa. We have forgiven over $2 billion in other debt payments owing to the Government of Canada. And on January 1, 2001, we also stopped collecting interest owing on the remaining debt from eight African Heavily Indebted Poor Countries who have committed to reform.

And I am very proud to say that since 1986, all of Canada's development assistance has been on a grant-only basis. Commitment to the new partnership is also evident around the G8 table. As the NEPAD asserts: "The continued marginalization of Africa from the globalization process and the social exclusion of the vast majority of its peoples constitute a serious threat to global security." G8 leaders understand well that a cohesive and prosperous Africa—an Africa with a brighter future—means a more prosperous and secure world. At Genoa [Italy, in 2001] we resolved to work with committed African leaders to help build and expand a new partnership, through the development of a concrete Africa Action Plan in response to the NEPAD. Discussions with G8 and African leaders are going well. And I am confident that our Africa Action Plan will help set a new course.

While optimistic about the outcome of the G8 deliberations, I would caution that neither the NEPAD nor the G8 Africa Action Plan should be looked upon as pledging documents or as quick fixes. In December [2001], our government set aside $500 million in support of the G8 Africa Action Plan. And at Monterrey [an international summit on poverty in March 2002], I announced that Canadian international assistance will increase by at least 8% per year in the years to come, which should result in our doubling our current aid performance in eight or nine years. Much of it will be for Africa. . . .

We have also received welcome news from the European Union and the United States about dramatic increases in their development assistance commitments—increases that will add about 50 billion U.S. dollars in aid to developing countries. Again, much of this will be directed to the assistance of African partners. But as partners we must remain realistic in our expectations. Despite these new commitments our African partners should not think of the G8 Africa

Action Plan primarily in terms of money, for it promises more than that. For our part, the G8 cannot reasonably expect the political and economic changes called for in the NEPAD to be achieved overnight. The economic marginalization of Africa was not a sudden catastrophe, but rather the result of generations of decline. A decline which has left a legacy of dashed hopes and fostered a good deal of mutual skepticism.

But have no doubt. The millstones of despair that have weighed down the people of Africa for too long will be lifted. They will know a brighter future. African leaders who fully commit to NEPAD will have the satisfaction of inspiring real hope and of making a real difference in the lives of their people. My friends, we are embarking on an historic journey of renewal. One of uncertain length but of certain destination. One that we will make together. As equals. In solidarity. Committed to the renewal of this great continent and the flourishing of its people.

> "*[The New Partnership for Africa's Development] suffers from some glaring gaps and weaknesses that unless corrected, will undermine the entire initiative.*"

The Initiatives Being Devised by Africans Are Significantly Flawed

Adotei Akwei

NEPAD, or the New Partnership for Africa's Development, is a political and economic program developed by African governments as a way of ending poverty and making Africa part of the global economy. In the following viewpoint Adotei Akwei maintains that NEPAD needs significant revisions if it is to successfully improve political, economic, and social conditions in Africa. According to Akwei, NEPAD is seriously flawed because it does not adequately address issues such as human rights and the critical need for free and fair elections. In Akwei's opinion NEPAD should be praised for its initiative and energy, but he claims it is not yet capable of improving the quality of life for Africans. Akwei is an employee of the African Advocacy Directory of Amnesty International, one of the world's leading human rights organizations.

As you read, consider the following questions:

1. According to Akwei, what two major human rights documents are ignored by NEPAD?
2. Why does the author believe it is essential for NEPAD to be debated and revised by the African people?

Adotei Akwei, testimony before the House Subcommittee on Africa, Committee on International Relations, Washington, DC, September 18, 2002.

Chairman [Edward R.] Royce and members of the Africa Subcommittee, on behalf of Amnesty International USA (AIUSA) I would like to thank you for holding these hearings on the New Partnership for Africa's Development (NEPAD) and for inviting AIUSA to testify. AIUSA appreciates the leadership and energy this committee has brought to critical issues like this and we look forward to continuing to work with you in the future.

Mr. Chairman, Amnesty International is a million member global movement dedicated to promoting the respect and protection of fundamental human rights. In the summer of 2000 at its bi-annual International Committee meeting in Dakar Senegal, Amnesty International delegates voted to change the organization's mandate to address grave human rights abuses be they economic and social or civil and political in nature. We therefore welcome this opportunity and hope that our comments and suggestions contribute positively to discussion on NEPAD's efforts to reduce poverty, achieve sustainable development, empower women, and encourage good governance in the economic political and legal sectors within the framework of promoting human rights.

Mr. Chairman, a . . . report by CNN made dramatically clear the need for innovative and dramatic action to address Africa's economic needs. The article stated that Africa's combined gross domestic product accounted for only .33% of the world's economy, the continent's external debt amounted to 65.1% of its GDP and that none of Africa's 53 countries was among the top 40 of the world's most competitive economies. When this is combined with wars in the Democratic Republic of the Congo, Sudan, the Mano River region of Guinea, Liberia and Sierra Leone, civil unrest and repression in Zimbabwe, Chad, Cameroon, Togo and potentially explosive elections . . . in Nigeria and Kenya, the urgency of the need for a change in approach becomes inescapable.

Amnesty International welcomes the energy and initiative behind NEPAD as well as its stated commitment to "deepening the culture of human rights." AI also welcomes NEPAD's stated commitment to focus on combating the proliferation of small arms, light weapons, and landmines and its goal of empowering African women.

As good a start as this is, however, NEPAD suffers from some glaring gaps and weaknesses that unless corrected, will undermine the entire initiative. Mr. Chairman, I would like to make some general comments and then focus my comments on the Democracy and Governance components and on the key missing element of NEPAD in its current state: civil society.

Human Rights Are Ignored

While human rights are referred to as core values that have been accepted as essential to good governance and sustainable development, the document in its current form focuses on the promotion of good governance including transparency, accountability, implying that human rights issues will be addressed as a matter of course. Given the document's primary objectives of attracting foreign investment and alleviating poverty, similar detail and focus to promoting the respect and protection of fundamental human rights would contribute greatly to the document's legitimacy and support within Africa and abroad for its democracy and human rights agenda.

NEPAD fails to build on existing principles and structures that would not only have acknowledged the efforts and progress made in defining and protecting human rights but would also facilitate NEPAD's implementation and further evolution. For example there is no reference to the African Charter on Human and Peoples Rights, which, along with the United Nations Universal Declaration on Human Rights, is ostensibly the continent's primary human rights document. There is also no reference to the African Commission, a body that is functional and has been monitoring the compliance of African governments to international human rights standards for over twenty years. NEPAD also does not acknowledge the Organization of African Unity's commitment to the establishment of an African Court during a period when the establishment of the International Criminal Court is one of the key examples of the globalization of the concepts of rights and accountability.

Once these key human rights principles are re-affirmed as being integral to NEPAD as well as to the newly launched

African Union, it will be essential that NEPAD set clear benchmarks for performance and set up mechanisms for independent, impartial monitoring and for enforcement. To date the only mechanism for review is the Peer Review Mechanism by African Heads of State. This proposal, while not fleshed out completely, has failed to alleviate concerns within African and international civil society that it will not be independent, impartial and aggressive in enforcing compliance by participating countries. If this is the case, how can NEPAD be expected to encourage investor confidence abroad when it is not seen as being serious in its commitment to police itself?

Recommendation:

1. NEPAD should refer to and be based on key human rights standards such as but not limited to:
   - The African Charter on Human and Peoples Rights
   - The African Charter on the Rights and Welfare of the Child
   - The OAU [Organization of African Unity] Convention Governing the Specific Aspects of Refugee Problems in Africa
   - The Convention for the Elimination of All Forms of Discrimination Against Women
   - The Universal Declaration on Human and Peoples Rights
   - The International Covenant on Social, Economic and Cultural Rights
   - The International Covenant on Civil and Political Rights

2. NEPAD should also incorporate other African standards and policies for human rights and Governance and move to develop and support the adoption and ratification of other important human rights documents such as:
   - The Additional Protocol to the African Charter on Human and Peoples Rights Establishing the African Court of Human and People Rights
   - The proposed Additional Protocol on Women's Rights to the African Charter on Human and Peoples Rights
   - The 1998 Johannesburg Declaration on Human Rights Defenders

3. A Human Rights Committee should be created under

NEPAD's Specialized Technical Committees Establishment and Composition to help ensure consistency and compliance to these international standards.

Civil Society Is Valuable

One of the most critical issues that challenges the heart of NEPAD's claims to aspire to good governance (in the form of transparency and consultation), and its claim of African ownership was the obvious and disappointing lack of input, and consultation with African civil society. Groups ranging from religious leaders to trade unions and human rights organizations correctly pointed out that the proposal was discussed more with Western donor government than with the very people NEPAD is supposed to benefit: Africans. This failure to consult and incorporate ideas from civil society suggest that African governments have still not accepted the legitimate and valuable role and contribution that African civil society can and must play if NEPAD is to have any chance of success. Arguments of a commitment to consultation following NEPAD's launch and in the fleshing out of the detailed plans of action only reinforce concerns of a dismissive view to larger questions and disagreements to NEPAD's tactics and strategy. It was not until two June of 2002 that African civil society associations and federations meeting to discuss the launch of the African Union and NEPAD were given the opportunity to comment directly on NEPAD and their recommendations are telling while they welcomed the interaction between the OAU and Continental Civil society organizations, they called on the NEPAD Implementation Committee *"to engage with African CSOs on a similar basis of full consultation and participation as done with regard to the launch of the AU"*.

The lack of recognition for African civil society is reinforced by virtue of the absence of any clear role for civil society in the plan's Peace, Security, Democracy and Political Governance initiative as drafted. This despite the existence of numerous documents acknowledging the critical role to be played by civil society in meeting Africa's challenges. This is even more ironic given the language in NEPAD exhorting individuals to mobilize in support of the initiative. While not everyone is by default a member of civil society, given their presence within the general public and their capacity to mobilize support and action, ignoring them suggests African government retain a low opinion of their ability to educate and mobilize the general public.

Recommendation:

1. It is essential that the NEPAD initiative be given to the African people, be they members of civil society or not, for discussion, debate, revision and re-consideration. This is not simply an exercise of due diligence, it is also imperative if NEPAD's commitments to transparency and good governance are to have any credibility whatsoever. This can be done through the holding of seminars and discussions using radio, TV, newspapers. This consultation should occur at all levels of society, including state and regional levels but even more importantly discussion on how this can be done should be held with civil society organizations and a plan developed with their input.

2. NEPAD should include members of civil society in its mechanisms such as the African Peer Review Mechanism (APRM) and should support civil society setting up their own monitoring system to monitor NEPAD, based in the five key countries that form the NEPAD Steering Committee as well as in Addis Ababa. These monitoring mechanisms would be to conduct advocacy, facilitate communication between civil society and NEPAD, disseminate information and monitor the performance of NEPAD member countries independently of the APRM. . . .

Promoting Democracy

Perhaps no issues, correctly or incorrectly dominate perceptions of Africa by the rest of the international community—in particular in donor countries—as much as perceptions of Africa being doomed to dictatorships, totalitarian governments, meaningless or repressive constitutions and impunity. While it is commonly accepted that higher levels of risk are associated with investing in emerging markets, having a democratic system of governance and the effective administration of justice and rule of law are clearly assets to encouraging private investment and foreign aid. While NEPAD appears to acknowledge this by having an initiative on Democracy and Governance Initiative, it fails abysmally to set goals and processes to underscore its commitment to monitor and police performance of participating countries.

NEPAD's Flaws

The most fundamental flaws of NEPAD [New Partnership for Africa's Development], which reproduce the central elements of the World Bank's *Can Africa Claim the Twenty-first Century?* and the United Nations Economic Commission for Africa's *Compact for African Recovery*, include:

- The neoliberal economic policy framework at the heart of the plan repeats the structural adjustment policy packages of the preceding two decades and overlooks the disastrous effects of those policies
- The fact that in spite of its proclaimed recognition of the central role of the African people to the plan, the African people have not played any part in the conception, design, and formulation of the NEPAD
- Notwithstanding its stated concerns for social and gender equity, it adopts the social and economic measures that have contributed to the marginalization of women

Patrick Bond, *Z Magazine*, February 2003.

NEPAD's Democracy and Governance Initiative states that NEPAD "undertakes to respect the global standards of democracy, which core components include political pluralism, allowing for the existence of several political parties and worker's unions, free, fair open and democratic elections periodically organized to enable the people to choose their leaders freely."

The initiative includes

A, commitments to be made by participating countries to create or consolidate basic governance processes and practices,

B, the undertaking by participating countries to take the lead in supporting initiatives that foster good governance,

C, the institutionalization of commitments to ensure that core values of the initiative are abided by

The proposal goes on to commit NEPAD to engage in

capacity building initiatives to help meet these goals by focusing administrative and civil services, strengthening parliamentary oversight, promoting participatory decision-making, implementing effective measures to fight corruption and undertaking judicial reform. The monitoring and review of these efforts is to be done by the Heads of State Forum, referred to as the African Peer Review Mechanism (APRM) following the July 2002 Durban conference on the launch of the African Union.

Again, NEPAD should have built on and incorporated existing standards and principles focusing on good governance, free and fair elections, the rights of political parties, and standards for fair, independent, impartial judicial systems that have been developed by the United Nations, the Organization of African Unity and the United Nations Economic Commission on Africa (ECA). It is also essential that along with these principles NEPAD incorporate the protection of human rights and creation of a safe, secure environment to its effort to promote democratic practices.

Free and Fair Elections

Another critical area that will have to be addressed promptly and forcefully will be the establishment of benchmarks for performance and details on effective enforcement. In 2002 alone elections that were widely condemned as being neither free nor fair were held in several countries including Zambia, Madagascar and Zimbabwe. Elections are scheduled for Kenya and Nigeria and in both countries serious concerns remain as to whether the elections will be conducted in a safe and secure environment and genuinely represent the will of the people. NEPAD's credibility will be seriously undermined if it does not clearly establish practices and codes of conduct that are consistent with international standards and act to enforce compliance.

At the same time the work and role of regional bodies created to promote good governance and democracy must be built on such as the election norms and standards promulgated in March 2001 by the Southern Africa Development Community Parliamentary Forum (SADC–PF) or the efforts of the South African, National Non-Government Organization.

As currently envisaged, the African Peer Review Mechanism (APRM) is limited to taking place once every three years, and to be conducted by peers of the government under review. The country will submit a report to be compared to evidence submitted by other sources including the ECA and country missions of eminent Africans selected by NEPAD heads of state.

Even as a tool to encourage investor confidence and to help firmly establish democratic values and practices, the APRM does not pass the test of independence. Limiting the review and evaluation of the performance of a government to other governments and to persons selected by governments will not convince anyone, either in Africa or abroad that a fair evaluation has taken place.

There is also no set of consequences that a country that fails to comply will be subjected to. Even if the best code of conduct is established adherence will be minimal if the consequences of non-compliance are not strong disincentives. The APRM was scheduled for further discussion and refinement at the June 2002 conference in Durban for the launch of the African Union. However few details have emerged to suggest that African heads of state understand that the issue is their accountability to their own people and not just their accountability to Western governments or even to each other.

Recommendation:

1. The APRM mechanism should be fully discussed and vetted with African civil society groups in an open and transparent manner.

2. NEPAD should include members of civil society in the African Peer Review Mechanism and should support civil society setting up their own monitoring system to monitor NEPAD, based in the five key countries that form the NEPAD Steering Committee as well as in Addis Ababa. These monitoring mechanisms would be to conduct advocacy, facilitate communication between civil society and NEPAD, disseminate information and monitor the performance of NEPAD member countries independently of the APRM.

3. NEPAD should incorporate accepted international and African standards on democratic practice including but

not limited to, free and fair elections, the rule of law and administration of justice, and the protection of fundamental human rights. Such standards would address the right to free association, assembly and speech and would [ensure] accountability for the security forces, all of which impact the creation of an environment that is conducive to democracy. . . .

Major Revision Is Needed

Mr. Chairman,

I have limited my comments to the areas of civil society, governance and democracy, issues that NEPAD has a stated commitment to. As I said at the beginning of my testimony AI welcomes the energy and initiative shown by the government involved in preparing the plan. That said the plan is at best a start that needs major re-thinking, discussion and revision both in many of its goals but even more importantly in its preparation and implementation. Any genuine action plan for development in Africa needs the participation of all sectors of African society.

At the same time if Africa is to be a full member of the global economy and community, then its leaders must acknowledge and incorporate global standards on human rights. It is our sincere hope that NEPAD become a process [that] facilitates respect for human rights and gender equality as it evolves and takes root in Africa.

"Africa's leaders need to recognize that free trade is the only way truly to empower impoverished Africans."

Free Trade Will Help Africa

Thompson Ayodele

Free trade is the best way to improve the lives of impoverished Africans, Thompson Ayodele contends in the following viewpoint. According to Ayodele, free trade will lead to peace between African countries, end corruption, and increase economic growth. He notes that in order for Africa to fully benefit from trade between African nations and other countries, its nations must eliminate barriers such as high tariffs and border restrictions. Ayodele is the coordinator of the Institute of Public Policy Analysis in Lagos, Nigeria.

As you read, consider the following questions:

1. According to Ayodele, how have wealthy countries slowed down economic development in Africa?
2. What is the average tariff rate in Africa, as stated by the author?
3. In the author's view, how do free markets make industries more efficient?

"**I**f you want something done well," goes the old saying, "do it yourself." After many years of looking to others to solve its problems, Africa is beginning to follow this advice—or so its leaders promise. Trade, not aid, is now being promoted by African heads of state as the primary driver of economic development, the one way to improve the lives of millions of impoverished Africans. But the current view is still focused too much on what can be done by rich countries, and too little on what needs to be done at home, by African governments themselves. As African leaders gather in Cancun [Mexico] for the World Trade Organization's [WTO] Fifth Ministerial Conference [in September 2003], the people of Africa hope that they will use this opportunity finally to commit to free trade on the continent.

External and Internal Problems

For many years, there has been a tendency, both inside and outside Africa, to blame the continent's woes on the policies of rich countries. While there is some truth to these allegations, the critics of wealthy nations never tell the full story. In one area, however, they are correct: Rich countries—especially the E.U. [European Union], the U.S., and Japan—restrict imports and subsidize exports of agricultural products, depressing world market prices for these goods and forcing Africans to import food that they themselves could grow more efficiently. Such policies harm Africa's farmers by reducing their profits and slowing economic development.

External factors are only a small part of the problem, however. Far more troublesome are the trade barriers African countries erect against one another, resulting in the inefficiency, lack of integration, and poverty that plague the continent. The long borders between African nations cause nothing but woe for millions of African traders. High tariffs and other restrictions turn what should be routine border checks into lengthy episodes involving harassment and kickbacks, with state officials demanding bribes to allow even the most basic goods to cross the border. Business trips that would otherwise take only a few hours eventually expand into an entire day or more. In the process, perishable goods spoil and valuables are stolen.

Political and Economic Benefits

Trade reforms can . . . help governments struggling to pursue broader economic reforms. Trade rules emphasize transparency, open competition, and the development of energetic private sectors; they resist corruption, red tape, and schemes for state economic planning and controls.

And open trade with Africa offers political benefits as well. Over time, economic liberty infuses the spirit of political liberty, as we have seen in Mexico under NAFTA [North American Free Trade Agreement].

Robert B. Zoellick, *Wall Street Journal*, May 23, 2001.

Excruciatingly high taxes are also to blame for the low levels of trade between African nations. While there is much talk of integrating various regions by creating free-trade zones, there has been little action to this end. The Abuja Treaty of 1994 [establishing the African Economic Community] provided for the phasing-out of trade barriers and the creation of a customs union with a uniform external tariff. But the average tariff rate in Africa is still extremely high: 19 percent, among the steepest in the world. The result is that exports from Senegal and Cameroon, for example, find their way directly into French markets, but not those of their African neighbors.

Free Trade Prevents Corruption

The easing of border restrictions to allow the free movement of goods within the region would enable Africa to avoid marginalization and to compete in global markets. In spite of low intra-Africa trade volume, many inward-looking leaders—in some cases, claiming a national-security emergency; in others, openly bowing to politically powerful local industries seeking protection from competition—are calling for outright border closure. Citing war as an excuse, Audu Ogbeh, the chairman of the ruling party in Nigeria, recently announced that the Nigerian government plans to shut permanently its border with neighboring West African countries. The people of Liberia and Nigeria know that trade between neighbors leads to peace; their leaders apparently have other priorities. When governments deny their people the right to trade, they simply encourage and perpetuate corruption. And the price of corruption is paid by those who can least afford it: poor consumers. For them, corruption increases the cost of living and makes their lives nothing short of miserable. Free trade is an effective tool against corruption, as it does not require goods to bribe their way into markets. Moreover, free markets improve industrial efficiency. Larger markets allow businesses to take advantage of economies of scale. Competition among producers forces uncompetitive industries and businesses to close up shop or change their operations to produce a better product. This is a great boon to consumers, who have access to high-quality goods at low prices. All of these measures will increase economic growth, thereby attracting both local and foreign investors.

When the world turns its attention to Africa, its focus is always on poverty. Africa's leaders need to recognize that free trade is the only way truly to empower impoverished Africans. Eliminating tariffs, quotas, and other policies that currently frustrate trade does not involve financial commitments or help from foreign governments: All that is required is for African leaders to give up their protection of local political interests.

As the world moves toward greater economic integration, Africa must not be found wanting. Many African countries joined the WTO in the name of liberalizing trade and promoting economic growth—and preventing a return to the era of trade barriers, economic nationalism, protectionism, and the myriad other measures that check the entrepreneurial spirit. African governments must now give the people of Africa the freedom to trade with one another. Until they are ready to do this, their continent will fall further and further behind the rest of the world.

*"An agenda of unfettered free trade . . .
becomes a mockery when 'freedom' means
unhindered access of multinational
corporations to African markets."*

Free Trade Will Not Help Africa

Leon P. Spencer

In May 2000 President Bill Clinton signed into law the African Growth and Opportunity Act (AGOA), legislation that eliminates quotas on the importation of some African goods in exchange for African nations eliminating barriers on American investment and trade. Although AGOA's supporters maintain that this bill will improve the economies of participating nations, Leon P. Spencer opines in the following viewpoint that free trade is unfair to Africans. According to Spencer, AGOA gives multinational corporations full access to African markets without granting African nations an equal opportunity in the American and global market. Spencer is the executive director of the Washington Office on Africa, a church-sponsored advocacy organization.

As you read, consider the following questions:

1. In Spencer's opinion, what act is unconscionable during a time of prosperity?
2. How has the United States shown its arrogance in regard to AGOA, according to the author?
3. According to Spencer, what role should the faith community play in aiding Africa?

Leon P. Spencer, "African Trade and the Gospel," *Off the Front Page*, vol. 1, June 2000, pp. 1–3. Reproduced by permission.

When Congress finally passed and President [Bill] Clinton signed the African Growth and Opportunity Act (AGOA) [in May 2000], a long-standing contentious trade debate ended on a whimper. The *Washington Post*, despite its substantial coverage of Congress, devoted less than two column inches to the story. Its key proponents continued to extol the great virtues of the act. African advocates, who had argued vociferously for passage and who had attacked those who did not agree, now spoke quietly that the bill might not be all they had hoped, but that it was a useful "first step." It might, they said, help the economies of some African nations.

You probably missed this debate altogether. Unless you are part of the textile or pharmaceutical industries, or have close links with Africa, or are active on economic justice issues, you likely heard nothing about this issue. And if you heard bits and pieces, they were unlikely to be riveting. Trade legislation isn't that way.

The Problems of Free Trade

But the debate over United States–African trade tells us something that we in the faith communities, grounded in a theology of justice and dignity, need to hear. I want to suggest three things: First, it is not anti-trade to speak of fair trade. Second, it is not blasphemy to suggest that many of the values underpinning today's capitalism—a word we tend to avoid these days—are radically opposed to those at the heart of the gospel message. And third, it is not right to declare that the economic perspectives of the U.S. should be the standard for the rest of the world.

First, fair trade. We need ways to exchange goods and services. Excessively restrictive practices and, certainly, corruption that exist in some African nations work against trade and appropriate economic growth. But an agenda of unfettered free trade—which the U.S. presents as the singular answer for economic growth worldwide and was the basic rationale for the Africa trade bill—becomes a mockery when "freedom" means unhindered access of multinational corporations to African markets where fledgling African businesses are struggling to survive. The income of many multinationals exceeds the gross domestic product of many African nations! In that context, being "free" to compete is no freedom at all.

What is fair is to recognize the extreme contrasts between the economy of the United States and the economies of African nations, and to provide means by which African economies are truly strengthened by their trade relations with the U.S. AGOA's aggressive answer was to press for African market access for U.S. goods while making a very modest and limited gesture at access of some African apparel to the U.S. When the *Wall Street Journal* wrote glowingly that the AGOA was "giving African access to the engines of the world economy," they were simply wrong.

Dignity Versus Profit

Second, capitalism and the gospel. This lively topic has been around for a long time. In the present context, what is critical is to contrast the gospel mandate for justice and human dignity for all people with an economic system whose inner logic is to place profit before people. It is, in a time of economic prosperity, simply unconscionable to impose upon an Africa that contains people living in extreme poverty, economic policies that undermine and indeed discourage such crucial public services as health and education, housing and sanitation. But the Africa trade bill followed this line, starting with a list of conditions for eligibility for AGOA's limited benefits that sounded very much like structural adjustment.[1]

Theologian Andrew Bradstock, writing . . . in *Church Times*, spoke of a God "for whom life, especially the life of the vulnerable, is to be valued above everything." He went on: "Any ideology or system placing a lesser value on human life therefore dishonors God." Well said.

The common "wisdom" today is that the free market is to be unquestioned. However, capitalism is a human creation. Where capitalism fails to affirm human worth and address human need our faith compels us to challenge the agenda ordained by those who possess wealth.

---

1. the economic policy that the International Monetary Fund requires of nations seeking debt restructuring

Trade Liberalization Hurts Africa

[A] U.N. Conference on Trade and Development ... in 1999 noted that rapid trade liberalization has contributed to the widening of the trade deficit in developing countries—which are located disproportionately in Africa. The report [by the UN Development Program] found that rapid trade liberalization led to a sharp increase in imports but that exports failed to keep pace. The problem is that trade liberalization can—and often does—cause imports to surge without a corresponding surge in exports. Not surprisingly this trend benefits the imperialist nations, the main source of imports and main proponents of trade liberalization.

Gerald Horne, *Political Affairs*, February 2000.

An Arrogant Nation

Third, the U.S. as the standard. For all our gifts as a people, our compassion and generosity, our government can be stunningly arrogant in its international affairs. The fundamental message of AGOA, for example, was that if an African nation wanted to trade with us, they had to play by our rules. The bill contained constant references to "market-led economic growth," the "private sector," and "economic reform," the latter a clear euphemism for the way the United States handles its economy. If an African nation failed to accept the U.S. approach, they were simply excluded.

Nowhere did we see signs of respect for the integrity of African nations to discern and implement economic policies appropriate to the needs of their people. If they tried to protect their modest industrial base from multinational corporations, they were wrong. If they tried to provide free health care and education for their people, they were wrong. If they sought to address out-of-control unemployment rates by employing people in the public sector, they were wrong. If, indeed, they tried to process some of their agricultural products themselves rather than exporting the raw product for process elsewhere, they were wrong (for reasons of tariffs and duties).

The Role of the Faith Community

We in the faith community need to be a consistent voice—domestically and internationally—for economic policies that deny profit as the sole criteria and that uphold a vision of a social good that is concerned with quality of life.

We need to draw a sharp distinction between free trade and fair trade. Between Africa and the U.S., fair trade is that which is mutually beneficial, which is sensitive to community life, which respects the contrasts between African and U.S. economies, and which grants special concern for the most vulnerable. We need to appreciate that trade of any sort is not the sole answer if the social and economic hopes of Africa are to be realized. The U.S. must juxtapose a more thoughtful trade agenda with continuing development aid and debt relief, a cause virtually all of our faith communities have embraced. And lastly, we need to be active participants ourselves in economic decision-making, and to encourage active participation by African civil society. Empowering people to articulate their own vision for the community and nation is well-grounded in our theology; it is important for us to find ways to be heard ourselves, and to ensure that our African sisters and brothers be heard in forums where decisions are made.

I would like to think that the AGOA may yet prove to a be first step—a modest step, but a step nevertheless—toward economic relationships between Africa and the United States that embrace human values. The alternative remains very real: that through the AGOA specifically and the U.S. economic might in general, we would be using poverty in Africa to force our own ideological free market agenda against the African longing for genuine and pervasive economic social development.

Which way the decision goes will be decided by whether, say, pharmaceutical corporations prevail or whether voices such as ours, who approach these issues from the definition of a common good and who bring faith to bear upon human worth and dignity, are truly heard. The gospel is good news for the community, not a proclamation for individual ambition. My prayer is that we will find the courage to say this, and by so doing, proclaim that which is counter to the prevailing economic message. Poverty is not going to go away until we do.

"In Africa [genetically modified] food could almost literally weed out poverty."

Genetically Modified Foods Will End Hunger in Africa

Florence Wambugu, interviewed by Fred Pearce

Genetically modified, or GM, foods are plants and animals that have been modified by the insertion of specific genes. Because these genes can improve crop yields while also making plants invulnerable to harmful insects, many people have argued that selling GM seeds to Africa would help end the problem of hunger. However, critics of the technology argue that these foods are unsafe and should not be sent to Africa. In the following viewpoint Florence Wambugu argues that GM crops are safe and beneficial. According to Wambugu, higher yields will make food more affordable and improve the quality of life of farmers. Wambugu is the director of the African regional office of the International Service for the Acquisition of Agri-Biotech Applications and an employee of Monsanto, one of the leaders in the development of GM foods. Fred Pearce is a regular contributor to *New Scientist*.

As you read, consider the following questions:

1. Why did the Green Revolution fail in Africa, according to Wambugu?
2. According to the author, why do many aid workers oppose the use of GM foods?
3. Why is the author unconcerned about the environmental lobby influencing Africans?

If you live in Europe or the US, genetically modified [GM] food might sound like a luxury. But for people in poor countries, it's the difference between a square meal and starvation, according to Florence Wambugu, one of Africa's leading plant geneticists. Would you expect anything else from someone who's been on the payroll of Monsanto? Perhaps not. Yet Wambugu is no puppet of agribusiness. She's the daughter of a subsistence farmer from Kenya who went into agricultural research to help farmers like her mother. "A hungry person is not a myth," she told Fred Pearce. "It's a person I know."

Fred Pearce: *Capaigners against GM food portray you as an apostle of Monsanto in Africa. Are you?*

Florence Wambugu: Some people say I am fighting for the company. But I say I am a stakeholder in this technology. It is twenty years of my life. I believe in the benefits it has for our people. So I fight for the credibility of the technology.

A Beneficial Technology

How can GM technology benefit the poor when it is an alien, expensive technology controlled by rich countries and large multinationals?

GM may be better for Africa than older technologies, like those of the Green Revolution.[1] In fact the Green Revolution, which failed in Africa, was alien because it came from the West. Africa's farmers had to be educated in the use of fertilisers, for example. But transgenic crops can get round that because the technology—to control insects, for instance—is packaged in the seed. GM also means higher yields. Right now maize yield in Africa is 1.7 tonnes per hectare; the global average is 4. But if you insert the Bt [Bacillus thuringiensis] gene as a genetic insecticide, 20 per cent of that shortfall comes back. I'm not saying that transgenics alone will solve all the problems. But it will lead to millions of tonnes more grain.

So unlike some people in Europe, you don't think GM technology is a bit of an expensive luxury?

1. referring to the dramatic increases in grain yields beginning in the 1960s, with the introduction of pesticides and high-yield grains

In Africa GM food could almost literally weed out poverty. In Europe, some people oppose crops with herbicide genes. In Africa most weeding is done by women—50 per cent of women's labour in Africa is tied up with weeding. Reducing that would have a major impact.

In developed countries food is getting cheaper because they use more and more technology, but in tropical Africa it is getting more expensive because it is all manually produced. People with a small salary spend almost all of it on food. If we can increase food productivity in rural areas it will bring the price of food down, and generate more money for investment to turn the wider economy round.

Surely what African farmers really need is fertilisers and better irrigation? Won't putting money into GM technology divert attention from these more basic needs?

I think that is like saying Africans don't need aircraft, we should go by road. Or that we should be denied computers until everybody has bought a typewriter and mastered it. We are part of a global community. Of course, we need to look at why existing agricultural technologies have had so little impact in Africa. Africa needs to pick and choose technologies, to learn which ones are compatible.

Don't you think it's right for Europe to be cautious? This is an untried technology and we don't know the risks.

Europeans tell us it is too dangerous. They tell us: "Africa, this is not for you. Keep off." You in Europe are entitled to your own opinion. But I think it is dangerous when you tell everyone else what to do.

Helping the Community

But you're not a farmer. What would a scientist from the capital city know about the needs of the rural poor?

My mother was a subsistence farmer and she was the inspiration for my career in agricultural research. We had a small farm with all kinds of crops. It provided our whole income as well as our food. Sometimes there was not enough, so I know about hunger. My mother would always look for ways to increase production. She would look for better seeds. We didn't have chemicals but she would use things like ashes to control insects. She made enough money to send me and my brothers and sisters to school. But it was not easy.

I have always wanted to use science to go back and make an impact on the communities that I came from. I've studied in many countries. I did my PhD in England. I did my post-doctoral degree in America and worked in the private sector there. But my heart never left the village. I decided to come back. People are dying of hunger in Kenya now, in Turkana. I don't want to go to international meetings and only see these problems on the television: I want to be part of it. A hungry person is not a myth, it's a person I know.

Why did you choose to focus your research on controlling the sweet-potato virus?

The sweet potato is a major staple crop. It is always there in the backyard if there is nothing else to eat. My mother grew it. I know it. Sweet-potato yields are very low in the tropics—a third that in China—largely because of the virus.

I worked at the University of Bath in Britain and did my field work in Kenya with farmers like my mother, who grew the crop. I wanted to solve a national problem. We were making little progress using traditional plant breeding. And there was a well-defined need to generate resistance to the virus that biotechnology could address.

Monsanto's Involvement

How did Monsanto enter the picture?

Monsanto had the technology to attack viruses and were looking for an opportunity to work on an African root or tu-ber crop. It offered to train and support someone and donate the intellectual property rights to Africa. It approached me. I went to the company and brought seven sweet-potato va-rieties familiar to Kenyan farmers. I had to learn everything from the beginning. Transferring the gene into the sweet potatoes took me about three years. Then we selected virus isolates from the fields in Kenya and sent them to Monsanto to test them on the sweet-potato varieties in the greenhouse. It's taken me ten years to reach to the point where we are about to begin field trials in Kenya.

It's very noble of Monsanto to donate the intellectual property to Africa. But other companies may not be so generous.

If a company comes here and inserts a gene into a local

variety, there is joint ownership. Kenyans should benefit. Of course, we need to be certain that the local genes are not just taken up and then sold back to us. That's why we need to enter into business partnerships. But we come to the table as stakeholders, not beggars. We tell companies: "You have the genes. We have the germ plasm. We know the fields. We know the insects and pests that are here. Let's work together." If we develop a victim mentality we become losers.

The Kenya Agricultural Research Institute has the intellectual property rights on behalf of the whole of Africa for the GM sweet potato. We are building a research infrastructure to develop it. This product now belongs to Kenya. It has no commercial value to Monsanto, except as PR. Next we will bring in transgenic cassava, using the products of public research. So again, no problem.

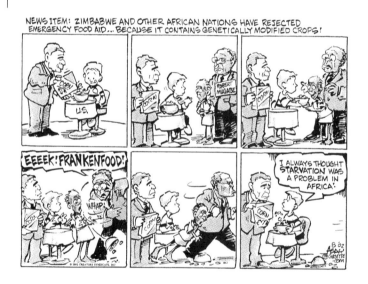

Asay. Copyright © 2002 by Creators Syndicate, Inc. Reproduced by permission.

So, what you're saying is that GM crops will not be as expensive as we're being led to believe.

Absolutely. I have worked on tissue-culture bananas, which are improved through biotechnology rather than conventional breeding. We show the farmers how you can purchase a product and make a profit to buy some more. The tissue-culture banana costs 100 shillings [85 pence], double the old price. People told us that farmers could not afford to buy them. But this is a myth, part of the donor mentality. There is money in rural areas if farmers can see the benefit.

We set about building confidence. We showed them some samples, and how to manage it, how the plants are uniform and vigorous and without disease. The demand for the new banana was unbelievable. Once they have seen the productivity of this material they have gone in and bought it with their own money.

One woman I know sold 48 bunches of the fruit in one day and made about US$500. She had never sold more than five bunches before—never made money like that in her life. She could afford to expand her kitchen. Now she has a team of 50 women. She is a consultant. We have put money into providing microfinance for the farmers. These farmers can eat more and sell more. We need this kind of impact to demonstrate biotechnology. This is the way we are going to turn Africa around.

The Opposition to GM Food

If GM is so successful, why do you think many aid agencies and even governments are so adamant that better food distribution is the answer to food shortages?

Some aid workers here—I won't name them—are being pushed into an anti-GM position from their European office. They're being brainwashed. We tell them we may not be the world's top scientists, and we know there are risks but we think we can manage them. When we bring the GM sweet potato here, we will be doing monitoring. We are not going to drop it and leave it. Many of them have come round. But they cannot tell their bosses in Europe.

But opponents of GM include some big-name scientists like Hans Herren, director of the International Centre of Insect Physiology and Ecology, a big agricultural research centre, based in Nairobi.

To me Hans has a typical European view. Hans will tell you he is not against GM but that not enough testing has taken place. Well, there has been ten years of testing. We know enough to continue. How are we going to know more if we ban field trials? What I am afraid of is being dictated to from Europe. You have surplus food in Europe. There is no real need for transgenic crops in Europe—nobody is hungry. But there is a real need and real hunger here.

Some scientists in the developing world think there is a hidden agenda behind Europe's stance on GM crops—an agenda to deprive poor countries of advanced technologies. What do you think?

I think the anti-biotechnology lobbyists are the only people benefiting out of this. Greenpeace is a $100 million company. To keep that budget you have to be doing something and doing it well. European people are having opinions forced on them through manipulation and half-truths about how dangerous the technology is.

Are you worried that the influence of the environmental lobby will extend to Africa?

It will not happen. We don't have the mass push of products coming from America. Things are coming one at a time. As we bring the transgenic sweet potato to market, we have enough time for people to debate rationally.

GM crops are unlikely to be introduced in Europe without strict long-term field testing of their environmental and health impacts. Is the regulatory regime in Africa developing along similar lines?

We have not compromised anything in regulation. You wouldn't believe the number of meetings that have taken place because there is so much money to help Africa build a regulatory system. When we applied to the government for a permit for the transgenic sweet potato field trials, ours was the first application. Apparently, a regulatory system did exist, but had never been used. It took two years to get the permit. But we now have it and field tests will begin here later this year. As a result of this process we have a regulatory system that is not brainwashed and which people respect. We haven't had mad cow disease here, after all.

*"Planting GM maize can . . . lead to the
contamination of GM genes into other
local maize varieties."*

Genetically Modified Foods Are Not the Best Way to Feed the Hungry

Seedling

Genetically modified (GM) foods are crops or animals whose natural characteristics have been altered by the insertion of genes from other species. GM crops are purported to have certain benefits, including higher crop yield; consequently, they may be the ideal solution to ending hunger in Africa. However, many people argue that GM foods will not benefit Africa. In the following viewpoint the magazine *Seedling* contends that African nations should not accept GM crops from America because such plants could threaten African agriculture. The magazine asserts that planting GM maize seeds could result in the contamination of local crops. *Seedling* argues that African nations should reject American food aid and find other ways to feed the hungry. *Seedling* is a quarterly publication offered by Genetic Resources Action International (GRAIN), an organization that promotes local agriculture.

As you read, consider the following questions:

1. In addition to inclement weather, what other factors have led to food problems in Africa, according to the author?
2. Why does the magazine believe milling is not a good alternative to planting GM seeds?
3. According to *Seedling*, what were the requirements established by the 1999 Food Aid Convention?

[T he] title of an article ["Better Dead than GM-Fed?"] in *The Economist* magazine of 23 September [2002] sums up the scorn that the US government has been heaping on governments and NGOs [nongovernmental organizations] resisting the US offers of shipments of genetically modified (GM) food to the hungry in Southern Africa. The *Economist* article claims that "Africans have two reasons for being wary of GM food aid: one silly, one slightly less so."

The "silly" one being that GM food is bad for human health and the other that GM maize could contaminate local varieties of maize. The tone of the article is a good reflection of how charged an issue GM food aid has become in the last few months.

Africa's Food Crisis

The crisis in Southern Africa affects Angola, Malawi, Zambia and Zimbabwe, as well as large numbers of people in Lesotho, Mozambique and Swaziland. It is estimated that, across the entire region, 9.4 million people already require immediate food assistance; a figure that [rose] to 16.3 million in early 2003. Adverse weather conditions are much to blame for the current crisis such as drought, erratic rains, floods and tornadoes over successive years causing drops in food production. Because of the long period of bad weather, many poorer farmers have nowhere to turn to find food. Other underlying factors have also reduced the ability of countries to feed themselves: political instability in Zimbabwe, a fragile peace in Angola, poor macro-economic performance in all countries in the region, inappropriate government policies, and the HIV/AIDS pandemic.

In emergency situations, food aid is mostly distributed by the World Food Programme (WFP), a United Nations body based in Rome. But the WFP and voluntary organisations only organise and distribute the food. It is national governments who provide the food aid, in particular the United States—the largest provider of food aid in the world—administered by the US Department for Agriculture (USDA) and the US Agency for International Development (US-AID). The effective early warning systems of NGOs working in Southern Africa had alerted the world to the impending food crisis in the region well in advance of the famine hitting hard. Malawi and Zimbabwe declared states of emergency at the end of February and the end of April [2002] respectively. By early June [2002] the first shipments of GM maize were arriving from the US. Zimbabwe was the first country to reject the maize, through fears of contamination of local maize varieties and the threat to the GM-free premium it commands for its agricultural exports. The maize was redirected to Malawi and Zambia.

The Danger of Contamination

Maize is grown as a staple throughout much of Southern Africa and there is a serious threat of the GM maize being planted and cross-pollinating with local varieties. According to the FAO [Food and Agriculture Organization of the United Nations], "Maize is known for its propensity to outcross, but this is less of a concern in southern Africa where there is no large genetic diversity of this crop." Southern Africa may not be a centre of origin for maize, like Mexico, but it is a centre of diversity for maize and such contamination could have very serious consequences. Maize has been grown all over Africa since the early colonial times. It was readily adopted by local farming communities because it grew rapidly and its cultivation was undemanding. Once dried, it stored well and germinated for several years after harvest. Some 54% of the maize-growing area in Africa is still planted to local varieties. This is because formalised breeding programmes have failed to produce 'improved' varieties that grow well in Africa. Farmers have had to rely on their own creativity to develop varieties that work. Over the several hundred years that maize has been grown in Africa, an impressive diversity has been created by farmers all over the continent.

The WFP, FAO and the US have shown little concern about the threat of contaminating local maize varieties. US-AID's Andrew Natsios claimed "Starving people do not plant seeds. They eat them!" While Natsios may know about famine relief, he doesn't appear to know farmers. However hungry, many of the recipients of the food aid will save some of that maize seed, albeit in small increments, to bury in the earth. Farmers can't stop themselves, because they are already thinking about next year's harvest and how to safeguard their food supply. Planting GM maize can then lead to the contamination of GM genes into other local maize varieties. This is exactly what happened in Mexico; the maize that has contaminated local varieties entered the country as food aid, with the intent that it would just be eaten, not planted.

The Health Effects of Genetic Engineering

Antibiotic resistance. Many GE foods are modified antibiotic resistant genes; people who eat them may become more susceptible to bacterial infections. Commenting on this problem, the British Medical Association said that antibiotic resistance is "one of the major public human health threats that will be faced in the 21st century."

Cancer. European scientists have also found that dairy products from animals treated with bovine growth hormone (rBGH) contain an insulin-like growth factor that may increase the risk of breast cancer, as well as prostate and colon cancer.

Immuno-suppression. Twenty-two leading scientists recently declared that animal test results linking genetically engineered foods to immuno-suppression are valid.

Turning Point Project, "GE Food," October 17, 1999.

African heads of state have recognised that maize seed will be planted, and some would be willing to accept GM food aid if it was milled, because it can only be eaten in that form. But USAID will not consider milling (either domestically before the grain leaves or in country when it arrives) because that would look like admitting that there is something wrong with the maize. Even the FAO does not seem to recognise how important milling is. It says that, "In the specific case of maize, processing techniques such as milling or heat treatment may be considered by governments to avoid inadvertent introduction of genetically modified seed. However, it is not UN policy that GM grain used for food, feed, or processing should necessarily require such treatments."

Milling is not a good option in any case: it dramatically reduces the shelf life of maize from ten months to three; increases transport and handling costs; increases the risk of infestation and increases delays. In addition, some countries like

Malawi do not have sufficient milling capacity in-country. In the end, some of the governments in the region have caved in to pressure to accept shipments of GM food aid. Zimbabwe has reversed its position and opened its doors to GM food, and Malawi and Mozambique have said they will accept GM maize so long as it is milled. Zambia is still saying no—against a formidable opponent, the United States.

Zambian Demands

The Kasisi Agricultural Training Centre and the Jesuit Centre for Theological Reflection have been at the forefront of NGOs in Zambia supporting their government's controversial position on food aid. They say that the current push by some relief food providers for African countries such as Zambia to accept the GM foods without any questions is neither honest nor fair. "As church groups with close connections with the suffering hungry people in Zambia, we recognise the seriousness of the current food situation in the country. The GM question is not for us an academic issue or a political debate but a matter of life and death for our sisters and brothers." These groups make two demands:

- That the Zambian government acts swiftly and openly to source and distribute non-GM food.
- That Zambia's cooperating partners should respond generously to the needs of the Zambian people and not politicise the issue or force Zambia to accept what it does not want.

In response to the criticisms waged by governments and NGOs, USAID accused these groups of endangering the lives of millions of people in Southern Africa by encouraging local governments to reject GM food aid. "The Bush administration is not going to sit there and let these groups kill millions of poor people in southern Africa through their ideological campaign," Natsios told the *Washington Times* in August. But let us take a closer look at the extent of the US's concern for the hungry in South Africa:

- The US says it cannot provide guaranteed GM-free maize because there is no requirement in place to separate GM and non-GM grains in the US. Strange that a 2001 American Corn Growers Association survey showed that more than 50% of US elevators can and do segregate GM and non-GM grains. The US position is one of choice, not necessity.

- US aid comes with strings attached. It either donates foodstuffs or it ties its monetary aid to the purchase of US produce. This is despite being a signatory of the 1999 Food Aid Convention, which recognises that food aid should be bought from the most cost effective source, be culturally acceptable and if possible purchased locally so that regional markets do not suffer. Cash is widely acknowledged to be the most effective form of food aid. It enables food supplies to be obtained locally and more quickly, supporting local economies and giving some possibility of ending the reliance on food handouts.

- The US introduced Public Law 480 to ensure that "commodities will not be made available [for food aid] unless the distribution will not interfere with domestic production or marketing."

- The US boasts that "The principal beneficiary of America's foreign assistance programs has always been the United States" and that its "foreign assistance programmes have helped create major markets for agricultural goods." USAID also states that one of its roles is to "integrate GM into local food systems."

- The US refuses to mill the GM maize even though African countries facing famine have requested this.

"I have heard . . . that people may become dependent on us for food. I know that was not supposed to be good news. To me that was good news, because before people can do anything they have got to eat. And if you are looking for a way to get people to lean on you and to be dependent on you, in terms of their cooperation with you, it seems to me that food dependence would be terrific."

Senator Hubert H. Humphrey, in naming US Public Law 480 the "Food for Peace" program, *Wall Street Journal*, May 7, 1982.

The US has persistently refused to respect Africa's concerns and requests regarding food aid. It is working to its own agenda, taking the attitude that countries in crisis should be grateful for whatever they are offered. The UN has not helped. The FAO has taken the line that GM food is safe, that contamination will not be a problem and, in so many words, that governments will be acting irresponsibly if they don't accept GM food aid. The WFP recently admitted that since 1996 food aid distributed to the South contained GM material and none of the countries who received the food aid—India, Colombia, Guatemala and many African countries—were informed. Since 1996 most developing countries have made it very clear, in negotiations on international biosafety rules, that they want to be told in advance about GM imports.

More than One Solution

Though it may not be easy and it may be more expensive in the short term, there are other ways to feed the hungry. Before March 2003, between 1 and 2 million tonnes of grain will be needed in emergency food aid. The FAO estimates that 1.16 million tonnes are available in countries as close as Kenya, Tanzania, Uganda and South Africa. Devinder Sharma suggests that India's 65 million tonnes of non-GM food grain stockpiles might also be a good source. Even acknowledging that there are a lot of different factors and logjams to consider, it just doesn't seem it should be that hard, if the political will is there. As Jean Ziegler, the UN special investigator on the right to food has said, "There is plenty of natural, normal good food in the world to nourish the double of humanity."

Periodical Bibliography

The following articles have been selected to supplement the diverse views presented in this chapter.

Kwame Anthony Appiah and Henry Louis Gates Jr. — "Africa Can Regain Its Glory," *Wall Street Journal*, January 28, 2000.

Peter Beinart — "Armies of Compassion?" *New Republic*, August 18, 2003.

Charles M. Benbrook — "Sowing Seeds of Destruction," *New York Times*, July 11, 2003.

Patrick Bond — "Cultivating African Anti-Capitalism," *Z Magazine*, February 2003.

F.W. de Klerk — "Africa Must Help Africa," *Wall Street Journal*, August 22, 2003.

Economist — "Better Dead than GM-Fed?" September 21, 2002.

Gerald Horne — "Africa Today," *Political Affairs*, March 2001.

Mike Lynch — "Road Show," *Reason*, August 2002.

David Masci — "Aiding Africa," *CQ Researcher*, August 29, 2003.

Marina Ottaway — "An End to Africa's Wars," *Harvard International Review*, Winter 2001.

Preeti Patel — "The Challenge of Peacekeeping in Africa," *Contemporary Review*, September 2001.

Jim Peron — "The Sorry Record of Foreign Aid in Africa," *Ideas on Liberty*, August 2001.

Wole Soyinka — "What New Kind of Monster Has Been Born in Africa?" *Los Angeles Times*, May 17, 2000.

Srdja Trifkovic — "Out of Africa," *Chronicles*, September 2003.

Robert B. Zoellick — "Trade Helps Africans Help Themselves," *Wall Street Journal*, May 23, 2001.

CHAPTER 4

How Can Africa's Wild Lands Be Preserved?

Chapter Preface

Africa is home to some of the world's most majestic and beloved animals. However, many of these species are endangered and at risk of becoming extinct. While conservationists fear for the fate of these animals, the rising population of one at-risk species, the African rhinoceros, suggests that there may be hope for Africa's wildlife.

In 1996 only ten thousand rhinos existed worldwide, less than 15 percent of the rhino population of 1970. The bulk of the surviving rhinos in 1996 were white rhinos, while less than twenty-five hundred were black rhinos; both species are native to Africa. This decimation of the rhinoceros population was due to the rise in poaching—hunters sought the rhinoceros for its horn, which was desired throughout Asia, Africa, and the Middle East for its use in traditional medicine, its purported aphrodisiac qualities, and its cachet (wealthy men in the Middle East often use rhinoceros horns as dagger handles). The rising price of oil in the 1970s made Middle Easterners wealthier and thus increased the demand for these horns, a situation that led to a two-decade decline in the rhinoceros population.

By 2001, the news was considerably brighter. According to the African Wildlife Foundation, the number of white rhinos had reached 11,670, while black rhinos totaled around three thousand. A press release by the World Wildlife Fund observes that this rise in the rhinoceros population is the result of several factors, including "conservation efforts involving government agencies, local communities, nongovernmental organizations, and private landowners in such countries as South Africa, Namibia, Zimbabwe, Kenya, Swaziland, and Tanzania." For instance, in Zimbabwe some private landowners have joined together to develop conservancies where rhinoceroses can be safely guarded, while South Africa uses monitoring programs to keep track of its black rhinoceros population.

However, while the number of black rhinoceroses has increased, the species is still vulnerable. Despite government efforts, poaching remains a significant problem. The most promising solution was devised in Kenya, which has established protected areas for its black rhinoceroses, where they live surrounded by electric fences and other antipoaching security devices. As a result of these sanctuaries, the black rhinoceros population in Kenya has increased by 5 percent annually.

Rhinoceroses are one of the species that makes Africa's wilderness special in the eyes of many. In the following chapter the authors debate ways to ensure that African animals such as rhinos can continue to thrive. Whether through sanctuaries, tourism, or even hunting, steps must be taken to ensure that these animals do not become mere memories.

"Trade bans are detrimental to elephants and other species."

Permitting Limited Trade in Ivory Will Help Protect Elephants

Michael De Alessi

In 1989 the Convention on International Trade in Endangered Species (CITES), an organization sponsored by the United Nations, adopted a ban on trade in elephant ivory in the hope that a ban would help protect the elephant population. Thirteen years later, CITES voted to lift the ban partially. While opponents of CITES's decision fear that limited trade may lead to a rise in poaching, Michael De Alessi contends in the following viewpoint that the ivory trade will help protect Africa's elephants. He argues that allowing limited sales of ivory will encourage Africans to view elephants not as destructive nuisances but as a source of income. De Alessi is the director of natural resource policy for the Reason Foundation, a libertarian organization.

As you read, consider the following questions:
1. According to the author, on what premise did the Convention on International Trade in Endangered Species base its decision to ban trade outright?
2. What is the carrying capacity for elephants in Zimbabwe, according to De Alessi?
3. In the author's view, what is the focus of Western conservative initiatives?

What is the best way to protect endangered species? Is it better to try to devalue those species by banning trade in products derived from them, or is it better to embrace markets and property rights that create positive incentives for stewardship? Every couple of years the debate surrounding this question crystallizes around elephant protection and the international ivory trade. Lately, markets, not mandates, seem to be gaining as the best approach to protect elephants, as well as the human populations that need natural resources to raise their quality of life. The reality is that in much of the world the desperation generated by poverty poses the greatest threat to endangered species survival.

The UN-sponsored Convention on International Trade in Endangered Species, or CITES, has been around since 1973, and a ban on trade in elephant ivory was adopted by the Convention in 1989. The ivory ban did succeed in reducing the demand for ivory in Western countries, but not in Asia. So poaching has continued.

Ironically, by succeeding in the West, the ivory ban failed in a different manner. CITES started out as an effort to regulate trade, but quickly moved on to outright trade bans on the premise that destroying the economic value of species will aid in their survival. Despite much evidence to the contrary, non-governmental organizations (NGOs) in Kenya and in wealthy Western countries like the US and Europe have promoted this view. But especially in poor countries where many of the world's endangered species live, those species that do not pay their way will be quickly replaced by something else that does, such as agriculture.

Conservation and Commerce

These realities don't stop radical environmentalists from having a field day whenever illegal products are found for sale, which they inevitably are (has any prohibition really been successful?). For example, the World Society for the Protection of Animals (WSPA) recently published a report that claimed that its own operatives "easily obtained illegal bear bile products from China at 67 percent of Chinese medicine shops surveyed in Montreal, Toronto, and Vancouver." The report offers an opportunity for the requisite hand-wringing over "putting a price on the head of every living bear"—a nice sound bite which does little to—help the bears, since the only result of stricter enforcement would be higher prices.

But even the "moral victories" of endangered species trade bans are wearing thin, as southern African states with growing elephant populations and rampant poverty have sought revenues from their stockpiles of elephant ivory (mostly from natural deaths or conservation-minded culls) to plow back into conservation and rural development. Some African nations do have depleted elephant populations, but many, especially in southern Africa, have the opposite problem. In Zimbabwe, for example, the estimated carrying capacity of the elephant population is around 30,000 animals; the current population is over three times that number, resulting in serious environmental degradation.

Still, for many people, the announcement [in 2002] that some southern African nations would be allowed to sell a limited amount of elephant ivory surely evoked anachronistic images of gruff, mustachioed colonials from the heydays of hunting. In 2003, however, nothing could be further from the truth. The reality is that combining conservation and commerce offers the greatest hope for improving the lot of both people *and* wildlife in the developing world.

The CITES Proposal

The vote to allow some ivory sales (but not others) that took place at the November 2002 CITES meeting in Santiago, Chile, was bolstered by both Canadian and US support, something past ivory proposals have not had. The United States has traditionally been one of the staunchest opponents of any and all international trade in elephant ivory, and Canada has not been far behind. Even the European Parliament, which passed a resolution urging its CITES negotiators to reject the African proposals, eventually abstained from the elephant votes. The change of heart seems to indicate an important shift in international conservation efforts, toward positive incentives for species and habitat conservation and away from prohibitions on trade in wildlife that have been the norm for the last 20 years.

Specifically, Botswana, Namibia, and South Africa will be

allowed one-off ivory sales of 20 metric tons (mt), 10mt, and 30mt respectively. This is the second time that CITES has permitted such a one-off sale. In 1999, Botswana, Namibia, and Zimbabwe sold almost 50 metric tons of ivory to Japan for about $5 million. Zimbabwe had another proposal this time as well, but chaos and corruption in that country left international observers unconvinced that the sales could be properly monitored.

Preventing a Bleak Future

Through CITES [the Convention on International Trade in Endangered Species], the international community has shown no respect for southern Africa in the elephant debate. Successful conservation has been punished and the goal posts have repeatedly been moved.

Southern Africa has a legitimate point of view, which is that a controlled, legal ivory trade from the region . . . need not result in increased poaching in other countries or regions. Trade controls are in place, and deserve to be tested on an experimental basis.

If they are not, the future for elephants looks bleak. The ivory ban, which has been in place for six years, is beginning to come apart at the seams, and human/elephant conflict is escalating.

Breaking the elephant impasse is essential to the future of CITES. The time is therefore right to reintroduce a legal trade in ivory. If it works, the impasse will be ended and everyone will benefit.

WildNet Africa, "Arguments for Re-opening Trade in African Elephant Products." www.wildnetafrica.com.

Even if CITES succeeded in destroying the positive value of species such as elephants, then all that would be left would be their negative value. Poor Africans most often bear the brunt of Western conservation initiatives, which focus on protecting elephants rather than elephant habitat, a far more important factor in ensuring elephant survival. And so, despite trampling crops and humans, knocking houses over, and generally wreaking havoc, elephants are rarely viewed in Western countries as a nuisance to the people who live around them.

The idea that wildlife will be better off without any economic value may have some merit for species survival in a

National Park setting, but on communal lands or on private property it has the opposite effect. This points to another fatal flaw of the CITES ban approach. The best hope for the protection of wildlife, and especially endangered species, is the alleviation of poverty and the reform of domestic institutions that have encouraged poaching and habitat conversion—an area that CITES has no real jurisdiction over.

Turning Toward Sustainable Development

A number of southern African countries have moved to devolve control over wildlife to local, rural communities. The idea is to recognize that people will protect and conserve what they value. Despite corruption . . . , it has been a tremendous step in the right direction. Community conservation programs have led to fierce local protection of wildlife, and the view that wildlife habitat has value far beyond simply being potential farmland.

Some CITES officials have also started to recognize the importance of making life better for both people and wildlife. "CITES seeks to promote a healthier and more sustainable relationship between people and wildlife," said CITES Secretary-General Willem Wijnstekers. In addition, Linda Maltby, deputy head of the Canadian CITES delegation in Chile, said, "We support the idea of sustainable livelihoods." Good news if this means that Canada intends to support sustainable conservation through commerce.

While the move to support the limited sale of ivory is a welcome one, it remains to be seen whether there has really been any sea change in policy. After all, ivory imports into the United States will continue to be prohibited under both the Endangered Species Act and the African Elephant Conservation Act. Canada, for its part, has the even-more-incongruous-sounding Wild Animal and Plant Protection and Regulation of International and Interprovincial Trade Act (WAPPRIITA).

Still, the move to sell some elephant ivory could be the first step towards an acknowledgement that trade bans are detrimental to elephants and other species, and that conservation based on incentives, decentralization, and ownership is better for both people and elephants.

"Any legal international trade in ivory could result in the kind of catastrophe seen before the 1989 ivory ban."

Permitting Trade in Ivory Will Harm Elephants

Humane Society of the United States

In November 2002 the Convention on International Trade in Endangered Species (CITES), an organization sponsored by the United Nations, partially lifted a thirteen-year ban on trade in elephant ivory and permitted South Africa, Namibia, and Botswana to sell sixty tons of stockpiled tusks that had come from elephants that died of natural causes. In the following viewpoint, written prior to CITES's ruling, the Humane Society of the United States argues that lifting the ban would be catastrophic. According to the society, permitting limited sales of ivory could increase the demand for elephant tusks and therefore lead to a rise in poaching. The organization bases its belief on the fact that a similar increase occurred following a one-time export of ivory stockpiles in 1999. The Humane Society is an organization that aims to create a world in which animals are treated with respect and compassion.

As you read, consider the following questions:

1. In the view of the Humane Society, what do the nations that want the ivory ban lifted value?
2. Before 1989, what percentage of ivory in trade came from poached elephants, according to the Humane Society?

Confirming the worst fears of many animal protectionists, greed has won out over good judgment in the southern African nations of Botswana, Namibia, South Africa, Zambia, and Zimbabwe. These nations [have] made it clear to the international community that they value the money from the ivory trade more than they value the survival of already dwindling populations of elephants.

The five nations have submitted proposals to the Convention on International Trade in Endangered Species of Wild Fauna and Flora (CITES), asking to reduce international protections given to elephants within their borders and to trade internationally in stockpiled ivory. If the proposals are approved at the CITES meeting in November [2002] in Chile, elephant poaching could increase.[1]

The five nations are requesting permission to sell off their stockpiled ivory. They want to export a total of 87 metric tons of ivory at first, representing about 11,000 dead elephants. In addition, they want to export an additional 13 metric tons annually, equaling an additional 1,500 dead elephants each year. Moreover, they want to be able to export an unlimited number of tourist souvenirs each year.

A Catastrophic Proposal

Experts see no good coming from approving these proposals. "If the proposals are approved, it will make an already bad situation worse by confusing consumers as to the legality of ivory and by feeding the demand for ivory," says Dr. Teresa Telecky, director of The HSUS's [Human Society of the United States] Wildlife Trade Program. "As we've already seen, an increased demand for ivory will, in turn, spur an increase in elephant poaching in African and Asian countries that are ill-equipped to fend off poachers."

Any legal international trade in ivory could result in the kind of catastrophe seen before the 1989 ivory ban. Prior to 1989, all African elephant populations were listed on CITES Appendix II, which allowed a regulated trade. The ivory trade regulation scheme failed. At that time, over 90% of

1. In November 2002 the Convention on International Trade in Endangered Species (CITES) partially lifted the ban and permitted South Africa, Namibia, and Botswana to sell sixty tons of stockpiled tusks.

ivory in trade was from poached elephants. "If we've come to understand one thing, it's that international trade in ivory cannot be controlled, and that allowing any international trade, even on a one-time basis, has disastrous results for elephants," says Dr. Telecky.

Revenue from Live Elephants

The positive effects of the [ivory] ban have been manifold. Apart from the reduction in poaching and the gradual recovery of the elephant population, there have been other major benefits. We have begun to help our people to realise the economic potential of live elephants. The elephant is one of the major drawcards in African wildlife tourism and the revenue which can be earned by live elephants, for the benefit of our country as a whole, far outweighs any possible revenue from ivory trade. For instance we discovered that a single live elephant in our National Parks brings in revenue from tourism, within a period of three months only, the equivalent of the price of ivory of 30 dead elephants.

Abdul Shareef, speech before the Environmental Investigation Agency, October 17, 1996.

To ban the trade in ivory, the Parties to CITES placed all elephants—African and Asian—on Appendix I. In 1997, CITES agreed to move the elephant populations of Botswana, Namibia, and Zimbabwe back to Appendix II and to allow a one-time export of their stockpiles to Japan, which took place in 1999. Inspired by this turn of events, South Africa fought (and won) to have its elephants downlisted at the 2000 CITES meeting. But opposition from the majority of African countries put the lid on any further ivory trade.

A Surge in Illegal Activities

As soon as the first downlisting was allowed, both poaching and illegal trade in ivory surged, though neither has yet reached pre-ban levels. Between January 1, 2000, and May 21, 2002, more than 5.9 tonnes of ivory, 2,542 tusks, and 14,648 pieces of ivory have been seized worldwide—representing more than 2,000 dead elephants. During the same period, a minimum of 965 African elephants and 39 Asian elephants have been poached and their ivory tusks removed. Furthermore, unconfirmed reports indicate that as many as 200 elephants were killed in the Central African Republic in 2001.

It isn't only the elephant populations with decreased CITES protection that are targeted by poachers. Kenya's and India's elephants are listed in Appendix I, but they face threats from poaching whenever restrictions on the sale of ivory are eased. "Poachers in many countries increase activity whenever CITES ivory trade proposals are announced in order to stockpile ivory in anticipation that the international ivory trade will soon resume," Dr. Telecky says.

This means that nations that shortsightedly choose to make money off the corpses of their elephants jeopardize the success of those nations that choose to profit from live elephants. The money at stake for those nations in the latter category is considerable: In 1989, Kenya's elephants were worth an estimated $25 million in annual tourism revenue. Kenya and India, which have kept their elephants on Appendix I, report high elephant poaching levels in recent years. They have submitted a joint proposal for the CITES meeting that would return all African elephant populations to Appendix I.

Ivory markets are flourishing. A recent investigation of South and Southeast Asian ivory markets, by researchers Esmond Martin and Dan Stiles for Save the Elephants, found more than 105,000 ivory items for sale in 521 retail shops in the 17 towns and cities in eight countries surveyed. Tourists and business travelers—including those from Europe, the United States, and Asia—are the main customers. Over 85% of the items on sale were jewelry, which is relatively cheap and easy to smuggle. Ivory products sold in Asian markets are made from the ivory of both Asian and African elephants.

> "*Uganda's innovative tourism program . . . is demonstrating that effective collaboration between protected areas and communities may benefit both wildlife and people.*"

Tourism Can Help Preserve Africa's Wilderness

Greg Ringer

Uganda's tourism program is proof that African nations can find ways to protect their wild areas, Greg Ringer maintains in the following viewpoint. He contends that Uganda has garnered much-needed funds for conservation projects by offering visitors trips to see chimpanzees and endangered gorillas. Ringer acknowledges that some Ugandans are critical of these nature treks, but he asserts that Uganda can best preserve its exceptional biodiversity by using tourist dollars to fund critical conservation programs. Ringer is an author and a professor at the University of Oregon who specializes in international tourism and sustainable community development.

As you read, consider the following questions:
1. As explained by the author, what event destroyed Uganda's tourism industry?
2. What percentage of all bird species lives in Uganda, according to Ringer?
3. In the author's opinion, what is the most critical problem resulting from tourism?

Greg Ringer, "Gorilla Tourism: Uganda Uses Tourism to Recover from Decades of Violent Conflict," *Alternatives Journal: Canadian Environmental Ideas and Action*, vol. 28, Fall 2002. Copyright © 2002 by Alternatives, Inc., www.alternativesjournal.ca. Reproduced by permission of the publisher and the author.

More than three years after the murder of eight foreign tourists, kidnapped while on tour of Bwindi Impenetrable National Park in southwest Uganda [in 1999], the country is finally, albeit slowly and rather tenuously, experiencing a rebound in international travelers. Whereas only recently, adventure tourism referred to the possibility of abduction and death for foreign tourists, the term once again suggests the possibilities offered by a country whose national parks and protected areas remain among the world's most significant, culturally and ecologically.

East Africa has endured decades of ethnic violence, institutional mismanagement, international neglect, poverty and disease. Yet, improved political stability and openness, and aggressive tourism campaigns have fueled a boom in tourism within the region. As a result tourism, and more specifically culture- and nature-based tourism, is now one of the most important sectors in the regional economy, and governments throughout East Africa are busy (re)positioning themselves as international destinations.

Rebuilding Tourism in Uganda

As the Uganda example shows, tourism development can play an important role in sustaining local people, places and identities during a period of dynamic change from a country in conflict to a tourist destination. But as we shall see, this strategy is not without its risks.

Geographically centered in the heart of equatorial Africa, Uganda has long benefitted from its lush natural and cultural richness. The country was among the first in the region to market itself as a leisure and safari destination, and tourism was the fastest growing sector in the Ugandan economy in the 1960s. However, the violence and turmoil following the military coup by Idi Amin in January 1971 effectively destroyed the industry. Hotels in the national parks were ransacked and wildlife decimated by rebel soldiers who terrorized wardens, residents and tourists alike. Years of warfare followed before the widespread killings carried out by Amin and his successor, Milton Obote, ended in 1986 with the victory of guerilla forces, led by the current President of Uganda, Yoserwi Museveni.

Fully aware of the importance of tourism to the country's

economy and anxious to restore Uganda's prominence as a wildlife destination, the Museveni government rebuilt the international airport at Entebbe and contracted with Italian and other European companies to rehabilitate and build new tourist hotels in national parks. By the late 1990s, nearly 160,000 tourists were arriving each year to visit the country's parks, wildlife/forest reserves, and newly established safari lodges and camps, and the $6.6 million they spent annually was a significant source of income in a country whose gross national income per capita is only $488.

Following the March 1999 murders in Bwindi Impenetrable National Park, the number of visitors to Uganda dropped 95 percent before rebounding slightly in 2000, when 19,211 visitors toured the country's parks. But even the pre-attack numbers were only a fraction of those who visit other wildlife destinations in southeastern Africa, reflecting Uganda's diminished attraction as a tourist destination. The attacks, therefore, only added to the challenges of marketing a country where the "mega-charismatic" fauna— such as the lion, elephant, and Cape Buffalo—are few in numbers, having been hunted to near extinction in the civil wars waged by Amin and Obote, and where the country itself remains synonymous with ethnic genocide.

Nonetheless, the government of Uganda is keen to address the challenges of rebuilding the country's tourism industry, and a number of initiatives have been undertaken with funds from the UN Development Programme, USAID [U.S. Agency for International Development], the World Bank and the European Union. Under the premise that economic self-sufficiency is critical to social and ecological sustainability, these small-scale initiatives provide opportunities for Ugandans to participate more directly in tourism. By funding investments in conservation and community development activities, the collaborations enable Ugandans to strengthen their communities through environmentally oriented activities and tourism attractions.

Extraordinary Biodiversity

Uganda's protected areas reflect the nation's biodiversity, encompassing freshwater lakes and rivers, savannah grasslands, wetlands and swamps, tropical forests, and snow-topped vol-canic mountains. To manage and protect these natural areas, the Uganda National Parks Authority (later renamed the Uganda Wildlife Authority) was created in 1952 and given responsibility for managing the country's ten national parks, seven wildlife sanctuaries, ten wildlife reserves and 13 com-munity wildlife areas.

2001 Wildlife Survey, Uganda National Parks Recorded Wildlife Species

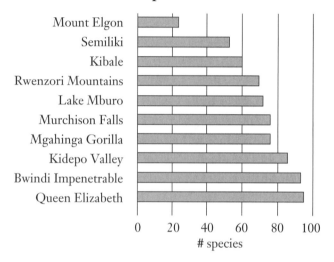

Greg Ringer, *Alternatives Journal*, Fall 2002.

In spite of the horrific slaughter of wildlife in the 1970s and 1980s, an extraordinary range of species remains within these environs, including almost half of the bird species known on the African continent and over ten percent of those on record throughout the entire world. In addition to the more than 1000 species of birds recorded on the National Heritage Database, of which 873 are found in Mgahinga Gorilla National Park alone, Uganda's parks and sanctuaries offer visitors a chance to see tree-climbing lions, giraffes, hyenas, hippos and chimpanzees, as well as the Sitatunga, an endangered species of ungulate. The cultural diversity is equally signifi-cant, reflecting the multiple ethnic traditions and lifestyles practiced by Uganda's population of 23.5 million people: from Bantu-speaking Bugandans whose kingdom, dominating much of central and southern Uganda, was restored by President Museveni when he took power, to the Niotics and the Nilo-Hamitics of the north and east.

Aware of the image problems associated with the country's troubled past, park and tourism officials have taken steps at both the local and national levels to remind international visitors of the unique tourist opportunities offered by Uganda and the link between tourism and conservation of the country's renowned natural and cultural capital. Undertaken independently or in collaboration with international agencies, such actions include the development of environmental education and cultural immersion programs in the national parks; whitewater rafting on the Nile River; mountain climbing on the snow-covered peaks of the Rwenzori Mountains (more popularly known as the "Mountains of the Moon"); and the one niche where Uganda can compete successfully with neighbouring countries: gorilla tourism.

Gorilla Tourism

Boosted by the continued fighting in the Congo and Rwanda, where gorilla treks remain ill-advised, Uganda has actively marketed the small population of mountain gorillas that inhabit Mgahinga Gorilla and Bwindi Impenetrable National Parks in the country's extreme southwest. Although there are only about 300 gorillas residing altogether in Uganda, this total represents almost half of the world's critically endangered population. As a result, nearly all of the approximately 800 tourists who visit the two parks each year are motivated solely by the chance for a rare encounter with a gorilla, and their trekking fees provide 90 percent of the Uganda Wildlife Authority's entire budget.

In the Mgahinga Gorilla National Park, tourists trek with Hutu and Tutsi rangers through a terrain of abandoned farmlands, secondary forests and old growth bamboo, only a few kilometres from Diane Fossey's former research station in Rwanda and the heavily armed Rwandan Patriotic Front soldiers who now patrol there. Because of the poaching and other threats along the shared borders, armed Ugandan park rangers now assume responsibility for the gorillas when they migrate through Mgahinga en route to the Congo's Parc National des Virunga and the Parc des Volcans in Rwanda.

The Uganda Wildlife Authority is also directly assisting local families forcibly evicted in 1991 from lands within Mgahinga Gorilla and Bwindi Impenetrable National Parks when access was restricted to better manage the gorillas and their endangered habitat. With the assistance of Peace Corps Volunteers, the Germany Animal Protection Society, and Care International, the agency decided to use interest earned from a $6.3-million Global Environmental Facility grant to fund community health and educational facilities, and to support enforcement and monitoring in the parks.

Through the project, which is still in the early stages, park staff provide environmental programs for local schools in neighbouring villages, and a community-owned campground and store operate immediately outside the gate to Mgahinga Gorilla National Park. As a result, local residents are increasingly supportive of the park's presence and efforts to protect the gorillas and other threatened species, such as the golden monkey and giant forest hog.

At the national level, the government organized the Uganda Community Tourism Association (UCOTA) in 1998 to support cultural tourism programs for visitors and residents alike. The group is funded, in part, by the US-based North Carolina Zoological Park, which provides technical and human support to the Uganda Wildlife Authority, as well as several British and Ugandan foundations, the Uganda Tourist Board, and a number of local Ugandan groups. In a joint initiative with the Kabaka (or titular king) of the Ugandan region of Buganda, UCOTA is constructing a heritage trail in the capital of Kampala for local school children. The trail will highlight the history of Uganda's 26 different ethnic groups. Village workshops on community tourism have also been conducted in a number of protected area communities, and an information centre for tourists and UCOTA members is planned near the offices of the Uganda Wildlife Authority.

These and other initiatives undertaken by the Ugandan Ministry of Tourism, Uganda Tourist Board, and the Uganda

Wildlife Authority have created a practical framework for both sustainable communities and tourism in Uganda. With their financial and technical support, local residents and resource managers now co-operate to provide a range of experiences for the visitor, from adventure hikes and cultural encounters to the new chimpanzee habituation experience introduced in Kibale National Park in 2002, where teams of volunteer trackers help accustom chimps to the presence of tourists.

The Challenges and Benefits

As tourism increases in Uganda, associated problems are coming to the fore. Perhaps most critical are the pressures placed on local ecosystems by recreational development in areas long isolated or "protected" by war. In Mgahinga Gorilla National Park, for instance, gorilla deaths from infections have increased along the border as a result of more frequent trekking groups and human contact, while the trash abandoned by nature hikers in the Rwenzori Mountains now constitutes a serious health problem.

In addition, there are increasing complaints among Ugandans regarding the trivialization of ethnic rituals for tourism, and the eviction of communities from lands historically theirs to create parks and other protected areas. Gender-related inequities remain cause for concern as well, particularly the rise in tourist-related prostitution and the transmission of HIV-AIDS. Furthermore, while women remain the primary producers of tourism handicrafts, the work is labour-intensive, and women are often required to travel great distances each day to find materials used in their goods and in daily life.

Despite these drawbacks, nature-based tourism is generally supported by Ugandans and their government (as evidenced by high levels of community participation and the priority placed on funding tourism projects in the annual budget). Though intermittent fighting continues along the country's borders with Rwanda and the Congo, there is growing confidence over the security situation and even optimistic projections that Uganda, once famed as the "pearl of Africa," may experience a moderate increase (6.2 to 6.4 percent) in tourism receipts in 2002.

Equally important, Uganda's innovative tourism program, emphasizing community revenue sharing and capacity building, environmental education, and sustainable use, is demonstrating that effective collaboration between protected areas and communities may benefit both wildlife and people, and in so doing, enable Ugandans to reconcile economics with ecology, visitor impact with sustainability, and pragmatism with vision. Though the challenges are considerable and, in many cases, beyond the control of local people and organizations, the Uganda experience makes clear the potential for tourism, if sensitively developed, to make a positive and long-lasting contribution to community and nature conservation in Africa.

"Just because something is marketed as 'ecotourism', doesn't necessarily mean that it supports long-term protection of the environment."

Tourism May Not Help Preserve Africa's Wilderness

Tourism Concern

In the following viewpoint Tourism Concern contends that tourism does not always protect the environment. In particular the organization is critical of vacations in environmentally sensitive areas in Africa and Latin America; such trips are believed by many people to be ecologically beneficial because the profits from this "ecotourism" can be used to fund conservation efforts. Tourism Concern maintains that while ecotourism can protect ecosystems if properly managed, more often it worsens the quality of life for the local residents and destroys the habitats of native animals. The organization further argues that the tourism industry is unwilling to change its policies in order to make ecotourism an effective solution to Africa's environmental problems. Tourism Concern is an organization based in England that works to reduce the environmental and social problems that stem from travel.

As you read, consider the following questions:

1. Ecotourism accounts for what percentage of international travel expenditures, according to the author?
2. According to Tourism Concern, how has ecotourism affected the lives of East Africans?
3. In the view of Patricia Barnett, what is the only way to make ecotourism beneficial?

E cotourism is a commonly used term internationally denoting 'nature tourism'. The term is used largely by the American public and tourism industry and less frequently by British tour operators.

The market for nature holidays has always been an important niche market in the tourism industry. Typical 'ecotourism' holidays include walking holidays, bird watching holidays, mountain trekking, rainforest trekking and safaris.

Ecotourism can be part of a more conventional holiday (day trips to areas of outstanding natural beauty) or can be a total holiday package where the tourist stays in a remote, rural environment for the duration of the holiday.

Ecotourism is a niche market: the World Tourism Organisation estimates that ecotourism represents between 2–4% of all international travel expenditure (the same size as the so-called MICE segment—Meetings, Incentive, Congresses and Exhibitions).

Ecotourism is presently seen as one of the most lucrative niche markets in the tourism industry as ecotourists are higher spenders than 'ordinary' mass tourists. High spending, nature-loving, responsible tourists are undoubtedly an attractive option for governments looking for ways of earning foreign exchange.

Economic and Environmental Benefits

Ecotourism is often seen by poor communities as one of the few livelihoods they have open to them. Communities whose people are living in poverty invariably find their young people migrate to urban centres because of the decline in traditional industries such as agriculture and fishing. Tourism (often 'ecotourism' if they are in remote areas) can prevent this urban drift and provide an essential alternative income.

Ecotourism, if managed properly, could also be an important means of protecting the world's rapidly disappearing ecosystems. If a natural area can be seen to have a higher financial worth as an ecotourism destination than alternative more damaging developments, ecologically important areas may be protected from deforestation, agricultural or housing development.

Ecotourism is not, however, necessarily 'sustainable tourism'.

Sustainable tourism is defined as: 'tourism development that meets the needs of the present without compromising the ability of future generations to meet their own needs'. This means taking into account social and local economic factors, as well as environmental management issues.

Need to Plan Carefully

Tourism will require careful planning in the future to avoid having further negative impacts on biodiversity. Many of the factors associated with biodiversity loss—land conversion, climate change, pollution—are also linked to tourism development. . . . Resources that are important for conserving biodiversity and supporting the livelihoods of local people, such as fresh water, are also affected by tourism development, and recognizing these links is important to managing tourism development into the future.

Conservation International and the UN Environment Programme, *Tourism and Biodiversity*, 2003.

"Tourism Concern is pleased that campaigning organisations in destination countries have pressurised the IYE [International Year of Tourism] to recognise that even ecotourism can have serious negative impacts on local people and environments and needs careful consideration," says Patricia Barnett, director of Tourism Concern. "All tourism needs to benefit local people and their environments, including 'ecotourism'."

Not Always Proenvironment

"While Tourism Concern is pleased that the impacts of tourism are being addressed by the international community through the International Year of Ecotourism, we feel that ecotourism is such a small part of the tourism industry it will not make a significant difference to the sustainability of the overall industry," Patricia Barnett says.

Tourism Concern has always pointed out that just because something is marketed as 'ecotourism', doesn't necessarily mean that it supports long-term protection of the environment. This is true even in countries which are well-known as ecotourism destinations like Belize or Costa Rica.

"Belize, for instance, is one of the world's best-known ecotourism capitals. However, it is something of a victim of its own success," says Patricia Barnett. "It now has a highly competitive tourism industry more interested in marketing a product than ensuring that it is environmentally sound, or that the people are benefiting from it. Local people are marginalised as outsiders buy up the land. Locals are angry that they can no longer access their own forests, which have been their natural home for generations and their islands are sold out to American ecotourism developers."

Tourism Concern also notes that as ecotourism is undefined, it falls prey to 'greenwash' marketing:

"Ecotourism can be whatever anyone wants. There is no internationally accepted definition of ecotourism and there is no certification system to abide by, or international monitoring body."

It also does not necessarily denote sustainability:

"The term can be used by anyone at anytime for anything from a small-scale locally-run rainforest lodge where the money goes to support a local community, to a large, luxury, foreign-owned resort which has little community involvement and uses masses of natural resources," says Patricia Barnett.

Tourism's vociferous appetite for basic resources—land, water and energy—has meant that the tourism industry and governments are increasingly finding themselves opposed over land rights and water rights by local people.

Ecotourists may even visit areas of national beauty and wildlife significance without realising that local people have been evicted from the area in order for ecotourism to be developed, as has happened in East Africa, India, Southern Africa and many other destinations.

Some Problems with Ecotourism

• Bolivia—environment: According to tour operators some self-described 'ecological hotels' around Lake Titicaca dump untreated wastewater into the lake. In the tropical Chapare region near Cochabamba, an immense area of jungle has been cleared to build a golf course for a five-star 'ecological hotel'. Bolivia, in fact, has no environmental standards for hotels (like many countries) and 'ecohotel' is a self-imposed title. (Source: *Latin American Press*)

    • Botswana—people: the remaining few hundred Bushmen

of the Central Kalahari are currently being forced off the land they have lived on for centuries by having their water supplies cut off. Intimidation and torture by wildlife officials has occurred. The Botswanan government has stated that (eco) tourists will not want to see 'primitive' people and the Bushmen lifestyle is not compatible with a developing country like Botswana. Most of the Bushmen are now living in desolate camps outside the parks, reliant on food aid. (Source: Survival)

• China—wildlife: Research on tourism's impact in Wolong Nature Reserve in Southwest China revealed that panda habitat was more rapidly destroyed than in areas not protected. Human population increased by 70% since the park was established to cater to the increased number of ecotourists. The number of pandas consequently dropped from 145 to 72 in 12 years. (Source: *Scientist* magazine)

• East Africa—people: Maasai and Samburu people in East Africa have been evicted from their lands in order for conservation and safari tourism to be developed. (Source: various, Tourism Concern)

• Thailand—environment, people: In April 2000, 100 angry villagers in Khao Sok national park in Surat Thani province, seized a bulldozer owned by the Royal Forestry Department and trunks of trees they had felled for construction of a 1000 sq. m parking lot, a 800m-long road, 10 toilets and concrete stairs leading to a pier in the park. Campaigners point out that villagers get arrested if they collect mushrooms in the forest, or corals in marine parks, yet various World Bank–funded projects are allowed to fell trees and make landscape alterations without prosecution, despite it being against national law. (Source: Tim-Team)

Paying Attention to Environmental Issues

Tourism Concern also feels that the question of how to manage a rapid increase in demand for ecotourism must be addressed by the organisers of the IYE in order that environments and communities will benefit from the promotional year and not be overcome or marginalised by it.

Finally, the concept of environmentally-sensitive tourism cannot be fully addressed without dealing with the environmental impact of air travel. Air travel is one of the main causes of global warming. "If tourists have to travel on several plane journeys in order to reach a remote ecotourism destination, can it be really be labelled as ecotourism?" says Patricia Barnett.

Is the tourism industry taking environmental issues seriously? Tourism Concern is very pleased that British tour operators and the British government have recently come together with British NGOs [nongovernmental organizations] to develop a 'Sustainable Tourism Initiative'. This is a strategy for the entire tourism industry, not just those involved in ecotourism. However, the commitment of the tourism industry to tackle these complex issues still seems to be limited.

"The mass tourism operators have learnt the language of sustainable tourism," says Patricia Barnett. "But little has really changed." Proof of this has been seen [since 2000] in relation to the tourism industry's response to the Balearic islands' decision to implement an ecotax of 62 pence per visitor per day.

The ecotax has been decided on in order to raise funds to correct the serious environmental damage done to the Balearics by the tourism boom of the last three decades and to protect fragile areas that are left.

The international tourism industry . . . has lobbied fiercely against it, saying that it would damage business. This flies in the face of . . . research, which revealed that 64% of people indicated they were prepared to pay an extra £10 to £25 for their holiday if it went towards environmental or social improvements.

"If the tourism industry is going to lobby against a small ecotax in a developed country, then we are not convinced that they are really committed to changing policies in support of the Year of Ecotourism. When it comes down to it, the tourism industry isn't willing to take the risk because it is so competitive and operates on such small profit margins," says Barnett.

Making Ecotourism Work

If ecotourism is to work, it needs to provide not only good conservation measures, but meaningful community participation too. Tourism Concern has established an International Fair Trade in Tourism Network, which brings together tourism operators, NGOs working in tourism and communities in destination areas, to exchange views and information on socially and environmentally-sound tourism. By using the concept of 'fair trade', which has been so successful with other 'products' such as tea, coffee, bananas and crafts, we are attempting to find a way to make the tourism 'product' more fairly traded.

Tourism Concern has also published a unique guidebook for travellers listing community tourism projects, The Community Tourism Guide, . . . many of which are ecotourism holidays.

Importantly, all of these projects are either run or managed by communities and the profits from tourism used for community development, such as water, education and health facilities.

"The only way that ecotourism can be truly beneficial is for it to be community-based. Some tour operators do work closely with local people in order for the communities to support their business and out of an honest desire to protect environments and optimise benefits to local people, but they are definitely in the minority," says Patricia Barnett.

"We hope that the International Year of Ecotourism will increase commitment amongst the tourism industry to be more community-focussed in their development of ecotourism."

"The poor populations of the world must make a living from their natural surroundings."

Local Control Will Best Protect Africa's Wilderness

James Shikwati

Africa will not be able to protect its native animals and wild areas unless local communities are given control over land, James Shikwati asserts in the following viewpoint. He claims that Africa has failed to conserve its wilderness because land is owned by governments, not the people. According to Shikwati, the government needs to recognize that impoverished Africans will be more willing to preserve their surroundings if they have a financial stake in wildlife conservation. He suggests that the government give local communities greater control by allowing them to co-own wildlife. Shikwati is the director of the Inter Region Economic Network, a Kenyan organization that encourages free market policies.

As you read, consider the following questions:
1. How did Africans view animals prior to colonialism, according to Shikwati?
2. According to the author, how did the antipoaching war affect local communities?
3. What does Shikwati consider immoral?

James Shikwati, "How to Protect People and Wildlife in Kenya: Right Now, Locals Are Out of the Loop," *PERC Reports*, March 2003. Copyright © 2003 by Property and Environment Research Center. Reproduced by permission.

Direct income from wildlife tourism contributes about 5 percent of Kenya's gross national product, accounting for just over a tenth of national wage employment and over a third of the nation's annual foreign exchange earnings. Yet the people who sacrifice to protect the source of this income—wildlife—receive little value from it.

All the wildlife in Kenya is owned or controlled by the government. Due to financial constraints and the conservation laws inherited at independence, the international conservation community has indirectly taken over this resource. The Kenya government's over-reliance on aid (an estimated $150 million from the international conservation community goes to Kenya Wildlife Service) has made it insensitive to the people's plight. In addition, whites and Asians hold senior positions in the conservation organizations. Most of the expert conservationists are whites from the West. Most of the safari companies and camps are owned by multinationals—Africans are secretaries, cooks, and drivers.

Popular notions suggest that Kenyan natives are keen on exterminating wildlife. Yet conservation and consumptive utilization were part of the African culture prior to colonialism. Africans co-existed with wildlife and would only kill them for defense and when they wanted to use their skins and meat. The Kiswahili word for wild animals is "Wanyama," from "Nyama," the Kiswahili word for meat. The Africans did not put animals into parks for protection; they protected themselves from the animals by putting up thorn fences or digging trenches around their homesteads.

Humans Versus Wildlife

After the scramble for Africa that saw imperialists control the continent, it became apparent to the foreign occupying forces that the pristine environment in Africa was being destroyed. The destruction was largely due to the white hunters and white occupation of the fertile African lands. The remaining land, either poor in fertility or prone to infestation by the tsetse fly and malaria-bearing mosquitoes, experienced conflict between humans and wildlife. That conflict continues.

Wildlife has invaded farmlands, destroyed crops, and killed people. In June 2002, in the Voi region, hungry lions killed fifty-four sheep. This led an angry Voi member of parliament to threaten to mobilize the community to kill one elephant for every shamba (farm) destroyed by animals. He cited the ineffectiveness of the Kenya Wildlife Service and called for its disbanding.

The livestock and crop losses caused by wildlife impact heavily on individual ranchers, pastoralists, and arable agriculturalists. The conflict between humans and animals is intense where forested parks border farmlands; this includes the Imenti, Nyeri, Trans Mara and Kwale districts. Other incidents occur where rangeland has pockets of agriculture such as Kimana, Leroghi and Taita districts.

On average, more than 15 people are killed by wild animals each year, with the highest number recorded at 55 people in 1992. According to the Kenya Wildlife Service, elephants cause 75 percent of human deaths from wildlife. The government offers 30,000 Kenya shillings ($389) as compensation for each person killed. The bureaucracy involved to get the compensation may take more than 10 years. This has made the locals rightly conclude that the government values wildlife more than people.

The Costs of Conservation

One study estimates that the net cost to the Kenyan economy from maintaining nearly 61,000 square kilometers (23,552 square miles) of land under protected areas is US $203 million. This is some 2.3 percent of gross domestic product, equivalent to supporting 4.2 million Kenyans.

During the antipoaching war between 1988 and 1999, when the government issued "shoot to kill" orders against poachers, many of those shot were poor rural folks. Instead of enlisting them in the fight against poachers, the government resorted to burning villages near the parks, as in Kora. The local communities were caught in the cross-fire between conservationists and wealthy government officials sponsoring poachers to get trophies to sell to their European and Asian accomplices.

The Maasai Mara National Reserve received US $26 million from tourism in 1988. Only 1 percent went to the local Maasai. Tourism firms received 45 percent, hotels 35 percent, shops 5 percent, taxes 5 percent, Narok Council and wages 5 percent respectively, according to the Intermediate Technology Development Group, a nonprofit organization. Only 2 percent of tourism industry profits go to the local people in Kenya, says this group. And the bulk of this tiny percentage goes to local leaders and those with capital and know-how to exploit the tourist market.

Environmental Colonialism

For at least a decade international conservationists based for the most part in southern and eastern Africa have led a strong movement for community-based natural resource management (CBNRM). The CBNRM advocates have argued that successful wildlife conservation requires the assistance of local African populations and have emphasized the importance of local economic benefits in order to create positive incentives for the protection of wildlife.

The efforts of such African conservationists, however, have often been undermined by their European and American counterparts. Financial contributors and other environmental supporters in Europe and the United States have found the myths of Africa more attractive than the realities. The international commitment to CBNRM so far has been more rhetorical than real. Although environmental colonialism is no longer as overt as it was in the original colonial era prior to the 1960s, it has continued in practice in the policies of many current African governments.

Robert H. Nelson, *Independent Review*, Summer 2003.

As [Benjamin] Aldrich-Moodie accurately observes, the poor populations of the world must make a living from their natural surroundings. Otherwise they will have little incentive to preserve these surroundings, including the wildlife that inhabits them. Only people who do not make a living in the vicinity of the wildlife reserves have the luxury of questioning whether or not human beings have the right to control wild animals.

According to Richard Stroup and John Baden, if property rights to a resource are not fully defined and enforceable, those who put a relatively low value on its use may use the resource without compensating anyone else. This is the case in Kenya. The government and western conservationists have ignored the local communities in their quest to manage the wildlife resource—even though the World Commission on Environment and Development of the United Nations in 1982 called for recognition of local communities' traditional rights to the land and resources they use to sustain their way of life.

When everyone owns wildlife—that is, when government owns it—no one will take care of it. The public or nonprofit decision maker who cannot personally gain from more efficient utilization of the wildlife resource will not be keen to minimize wastage.

Strengthen Local Power

What is urgently needed locally is the strengthening of the institutions of justice to ensure the rule of law and the devolution of property rights to the local communities. At the international level, it is important to have the western world listen to the plight of the people around the wildlife conservation areas. The former director of Kenya Wildlife Service, David Western, observed correctly that if villagers living around a park made money from wildlife, the park would in effect become the villagers' bank and the wild animals in the park their assets. This would provide a powerful incentive against poaching. People are not likely to rob their own bank.

The farming communities should be exposed to farming methods that increase yield per hectare in order to reduce competition for space with the wildlife. They should also be allowed to co-own wildlife around their farms and/or be entitled to shares in the parks, now owned by the government, around their farms. Landowners whose land the animals occupy outside official protected areas should be included in the Kenya Wildlife Service board of management. This representation will help check disputes between the government agency and the locals.

Another approach would be to decentralize the Kenya Wildlife Service into regional committees that are managed by elected representatives from the ranches, farmers, trust land, and government land representatives. An efficient licensing procedure for supplying locally caught game to restaurants would provide an incentive for local participation in conservation and encourage employment.

Locals should be well informed on wildlife and conservation issues. A network should be put in place to facilitate communication between the African Kenyans, the white Kenyans and external wildlife experts to stop the trend of outsiders dictating issues locally. A study is urgently needed to clarify issues on possible wildlife ownership and local responsibility for wildlife.

There is absolutely nothing immoral in having people own wildlife. It is immoral to have them trampled to death and their crops destroyed with no gain in sight. It is illogical to have people drown in poverty when they can profitably gain from wildlife.

"Through managed culling and hunting programs numbers can be kept under control."

Controlled Hunting Will Help Preserve Africa's Wildlife

Jens du Plessis

In the following viewpoint Jens du Plessis maintains that controlled hunting is the best way to protect Africa's wildlife. He argues that limited hunting and culling is necessary because overpopulation strains the carrying capacity of the species' habitats. In addition, du Plessis asserts, Africans can sell the culled animals' horns, bones, and skins to fund conservation efforts. Jens du Plessis is the founder of African Zebra, an online African market that sells wildlife products and arts and crafts. African Zebra publishes the online newsletter *African Herald*.

As you read, consider the following questions:

1. What is one of Africa's biggest dilemmas, in du Plessis's opinion?
2. According to the author, how many zebras are culled in Kenya each year?
3. How does conservation become self-sustaining, as explained by du Plessis?

One of Africa's major dilemmas is the fact that the Continent is rich in natural resources but poor in its development. Many of its natural wealth is exported, in raw or semi-raw form, to more developed countries to be converted into a variety of other products.

This is typically the case with its gold, its copper, its diamonds and many of its other minerals and raw materials, only then having to import the finished products at high cost.

Africa is known globally for its natural beauty and for its wildlife. The lion is commonly known as the King of the Jungle, there are no pretenders to the throne. Together with the majestic elephant, the pre-historic rhino, the sleek leopard and the crusty buffalo they make up what is known as the BIG FIVE. No other group of animals can rightfully claim that title, although they try.

Add to these the stately giraffe, the zebra—the horse in pajamas and the fleeting gazelle, to name a few and you have a wildlife kingdom that exists nowhere else in the world!

Preventing Over-Population

But the preservation of this kingdom comes at a cost. To preserve and conserve these animal populations require large areas of land, manpower and dedicated and qualified management. With the help of private enterprise the conservation of Africa's wildlife in many countries, especially in Southern Africa, has been very successful. In many ways, too successful, resulting in over-population in many of the species.

There is only so much land available, only so much water available, only so much food available.

While tourism brings many people to the sub-continent, generating income and work for the human population and funding conservation, at some point animal populations must be reduced to protect the ecology, to protect the species and to protect other species. As any livestock farmer will tell you, an area of land can only sustain so much life. Then numbers have to be reduced.

Through regular auctions and sales large numbers of animals arc sold to game farms, other game reserves and zoos all over the world. But again, only so many can be sold.

What happens to the rest?

187

Avoiding Unpleasant Deaths

Without hunting, wildlife managers have two alternatives: do nothing and allow elephants to die from starvation (as they did in Gonarezhou National Park in 1992), or employ park rangers to kill selected elephants, an unpleasant and expensive task that takes money from other wildlife protection measures. Either way, elephants will die. A better alternative . . . is for the government to sell hunting licenses to support conservation and development.

Richard Miniter, *Wall Street Journal*, July 17, 1997.

Through managed culling programs over-stocked populations are reduced. Through controlled hunting on private farms numbers are kept under control. In Kenya alone between 30,000 and 50,000 Burchell's zebras need to be culled every year. Botswana, with over 300,000 elephants, [has] run into serious problems with over-grazing and deforestation in many parts. The Kruger National Park, in South Africa, is at capacity with over 7,000 elephants and they are increasing at 7% per year.

Creating Income Through Conservation

In South Africa we believe in conservation through utilisation. With this we mean that we regard our wildlife as one of our natural resources, there to be preserved and utilised for the benefit of all, both animal and human.

Through managed culling and hunting programs numbers can be kept under control. And by using the culled animals' skins, their bones, their horns to generate income conservation can be improved further.

Many individuals and animal rights organisations raise their voices about the cruelty of killing the animals and would want the African countries to protect all and always. This is short-sighted and impractical for the very reasons I already mentioned. Even organisations such as the SPCA [Society of the Prevention of Cruelty to Animals] have to put down many of the animals in their care.

If they accept the necessity of controlling the animal populations, they believe that these culled animals must not be used for profit or gain. Please tell me: why not? Africa is not a rich continent and the cost of conservation rests squarely on the countries where these animals live. To fund conservation takes millions, if not billions, of dollars each year.

How must countries pay for this? By using the very natural resource [they are] protecting! It makes sense that conservation becomes largely self-sustaining.

Yes, we at African Zebra operate our Internet business for profit, as do most other businesses involved in the wildlife industry, and we do not apologise for that.

We do NOT believe in uncontrolled hunting, and senseless killing or in "canned" hunting to satisfy some ego-maniac's lust for glory.

For this very reason we are avid supporters of conservation. It protects our livelihood, while at the same time protects the beauty of our country and makes Southern Africa an attractive tourist destination.

Conservation without utilisation, has limited benefits—conservation with utilisation, benefits all.

> *"When [Africans] killed [animals], they did so with deep respect because they said that every animal had a spirit and you had to acknowledge it."*

An Understanding of African Tradition Is Needed to Preserve Africa's Wilderness

Ian Player

In the following viewpoint Ian Player argues that the best way to preserve Africa's wilderness is by returning to traditional ways of managing wild lands. Player explains that Africans traditionally lived in harmony with nature, unlike modern people, who are systematically destroying the wilderness. He contends that both African and non-African people need to acknowledge the scientific, spiritual, and cultural values that can be found only in Africa's wilderness areas. Player is the director of the Wilderness Foundation, a preservationist organization located in South Africa.

As you read, consider the following questions:
1. What did Player's work as a game ranger lead him to realize?
2. According to the author, to what do the Zulu names of the months refer?
3. In Player's opinion, what tradition can Africa reintroduce?

Ian Player, "In Defence of Wilderness," *Resurgence*, November/December 1997. Copyright © 1997 by Resurgence, Ltd., www.resurgence.org. Reproduced by permission.

All native peoples had places that were sacred: the Celts and their nemetons, the Ancient Greeks and their forests, the Africans, the native Americans, the Aborigines, all had sacred sites in wilderness that were looked after by the spirits and revered by people.

I must emphasize that there is a very big difference between a national park or a game reserve and a wilderness area. One can have a wilderness area within a park, but of wilderness someone once said, "It is where the moderns at least see what their ancestors knew in their nerves and their blood."

There are many values of wilderness: scientific, historical, educational, recreational and spiritual. . . .

Wilderness is both a geographical area and a philosophical idea. Magqubu Ntombela, my Zulu mentor, was a speaker at the first World Wilderness Congress, which was held in South Africa. Although he could not speak English and had to have an interpreter, he had his audience entranced when he spoke about the seasons of the year. It was quite clear that what modern people regard as wilderness the indigenous people saw as home.

Learning About Wildlife

I went to the Second World War at the age of seventeen. During the war I made a promise to myself to canoe from the city of Pietermaritzburg to the port of Durban, down the rivers that rise in the great Drakensberg mountains of KwaZulu-Natal.

This was my first experience of wilderness. The two rivers run through the Valley of a Thousand Hills. Day after day I paddled alone in deep gorges, sometimes caught in thunder and lightning storms that swept up the rivers. It took seven days to canoe the 110 miles and I entered a new world, and the beginning of an understanding of my relationship to the Earth. But one thing shocked me: I saw very few wild animals; in fact, only two grey duiker. That made me determined to try to do something about wildlife conservation.

I joined the Natal Parks Board in 1952 and served in all the game reserves of Zululand. Lake St. Lucia was my first station. In April and May, the pelicans arrive to breed and at the same time the great mullet shoals gather in their thousands, before moving down the lake on their journey to the sea. Sometimes when the crocodile went in amongst them at night the roar of the fish jumping would wake me. If you shone a light from a boat, so many mullet would jump into it that the boat could sink. My foot patrols took me over the dune forests to the beaches and the great bat caves. I fished for my own food and slept next to driftwood fires. Slowly the wilderness world was weaving its web over me.

Toles. Copyright © 1999 by *Buffalo News*. Reproduced by permission of Universal Press Syndicate.

Then I was posted to Ndumu game reserve on the Mozambique border, some of the wildest country left in South Africa. A friend sent me Laurens van der Post's book, *Venture to the Interior*. It made me aware that we, the Caucasians, had not acknowledged the noble soul of Africa. In fact, we attacked it in every possible technological way. We killed the people we called "the savages". My own great-grandfather was in the colonial army and was sent to shoot Bushpeople. The only thing that remains today of the Bushpeople in the Drakensberg mountains is a hundred miles of caves with their exquisite paintings. Sometimes I sit in them in the late afternoon and the evening, and in my imagination I can hear the Bushpeople talking. The paintings glow numinously, but the morning light shows the obscenities written by our own people on and above these wonderful works of art. You have to ask who is civilized?

Africa has always been regarded as a poor relation by the rest of the world. But Africa has made contributions that few people have taken time to think about.

The old Africa is almost gone. My work as a game ranger made me realize that humankind has a terrible power and is systematically wiping out species, destroying ecosystems and eliminating wilderness.

The Zulu Understanding of Nature

My own understanding of the mysteries of Africa came through Qumbu Magqubu Ntombela, a Zulu, who led me along the rhino, hippo and elephant trails in Mfolozi game reserve. These were the old hunting grounds of the early Zulu kings. I began to see the country through his eyes and learn how his culture had valued it. I learnt to appreciate how they respected the animals. Even when they killed them, they did so with deep respect because they said that every animal had a spirit and you had to acknowledge it. . . .

I grew to appreciate that this was a very great man. He became my leader, teacher and mentor.

He taught me the need to respect the whole natural world. He began by telling me the Zulu months of the year. Each Zulu name describes the changing season. April is the first nip of cold and people start making fires in their huts, and June is when the trees start to shed their leaves. July is the beginning of the wind that blows the leaves off the trees and the world is full of dust. In October the paths are covered by grass that has started to grow after the first rains. November is when the pumpkins become ripe and in December the wildebeest give birth to their calves.

I knew then that what Henry Miller had said was true: "The world is not to be put in order, the world is order incarnate. It is for us to put ourselves in unison with this order to know what is world order." In my forty-four years with Magqubu Ntombela I learned to know that he was in harmony with that world.

What remains of African wilderness is of the greatest importance because Africa can provide recreation in the true meaning of the word. To re-create something inside ourselves. This will give us the opportunity to build a stronger symbiotic relationship between Africa and the Western world. Africa can help the world, particularly spiritually. Amongst many people in the West there is a weariness caused by travel without a purpose. Instead of the pilgrimages we once were on, we travel to escape. Africa can reintroduce the tradition of pilgrimage and bring a new dimension to travel. To sleep beside lonely fires on the red earth in the African bush will connect us to a primeval part of ourselves.

In African wilderness there is an ancient spirit, said to be older than the human spirit. And it still survives in the vast, brooding acacia bushveld, in some of the remote mountains and along the wild coastlines. What we have in these wild lands are the most precious of our worldly gifts. But our wild country is terribly vulnerable, protected by a thin membrane, a caul that can be torn and rendered useless, frequently by the very people who are charged to look after it.

In my life I have tried to make allies and win over people to help us in this great battle for wild Africa. I was fortunate in my time to have wilderness areas set aside in Zululand. I have worked for forty years as a wildlife conservation officer and as a director with non-governmental wilderness organizations. Magqubu and I took over 1,000 people on wilderness treks. I wanted to make people appreciate the wilderness. I wanted them to be touched by the small remaining wild landscapes of Zululand. But without Magqubu Ntombela this would never have been possible. He was the inspiration, the teacher and the interpreter of the African land. . . .

Africa is a huge continent and many of the countries within it are in a convulsive uproar. It is, I believe, at its own pace slowly re-establishing its ancient pattern, and if the Western world could re-enforce the protection of real wilderness areas, this would be the best recompense for the colonial exploitations of the past.

Periodical Bibliography

The following articles have been selected to supplement the diverse views presented in this chapter.

Current Events	"Gorilla Warfare," February 21, 2003.
Economist	"Closing in for the Kill?" May 18, 2002.
Aliette K. Frank	"Caught in the Crossfire," *National Wildlife*, August/September 2002.
Rolf Hogan	"The Wildlife Trade," *UNESCO Courier*, July 2000.
Terra MacKinnon	"Savage Tastes," *Canadian Wildlife*, Winter 2002.
Kay Muir-Leresche and Robert H. Nelson	"Managing Wildlife in Southern Africa," *PERC Reports*, September 2001.
Robert H. Nelson	"Environmental Colonialism: 'Saving' Africa from Africans," *Independent Review*, Summer 2003.
Tom Nevin and Stephen Williams	"Protecting Africa's Greatest Asset," *African Business*, October 1999.
Michael Satchell	"Hunting to Extinction," *U.S. News & World Report*, October 9, 2000.
Virginia M. Sixeas	"The Cost of Ivory," *Environment*, April 2000.
Marilyn Berlin Snell	"Gorillas in the Crossfire," *Sierra*, November/December 2001.
Craig B. Stanford	"Gorilla Warfare," *Sciences*, July 1999.
UN Chronicle	"An Insight into Africa's Threatened Sea Turtles," March–May 2002.
David Western	"Conservation in a Human-Dominated World," *Issues in Science and Technology*, Spring 2000.
G. Pascal Zachary	"Bush Meat," *In These Times*, October 27, 2003.

For Further Discussion

Chapter 1

1. Of the three problems examined in this chapter—Africa's economic future, its prospects for democracy, and the continuing problem of racial prejudice—which do you think is the most serious? Is there a problem that was not addressed by the authors that you think has had a greater impact on Africa, and if so, what is that issue? Please explain your answers.

2. The two viewpoints on African democracy were written by North Americans, not Africans. Do you think that their perspective as outsiders makes Marina Ottaway and Richard Sandbrook better able to offer objective analysis of the quality of African democracy? Do you feel that their conclusions, whether positive or negative, show indications of Western condescension? Why or why not?

3. Alec Russell and James M. Statman offer opposing views on prejudice in South Africa. Whose argument do you find more convincing and why? What steps do you think could be taken in order to encourage racial harmony?

Chapter 2

1. While AIDS cannot be cured, combinations of medicines known as drug cocktails can extend and improve the quality of life for people with the ailment. Robert Weissman argues that pharmaceutical companies need to take steps in order to make these drug cocktails more affordable to Africans with AIDS. On the other hand, Siddhartha Mukherjee contends that reducing the costs of anti-AIDS drugs could be dangerous because HIV can mutate if the medicines are not taken properly. Whose argument do you find more convincing and why?

2. Nada Chaya and Kali-Ahset Amen contend that condoms are the best way to reduce the spread of AIDS in Africa. If you believe their conclusion is accurate, how do you think African society can most effectively encourage condom use? On the other hand, if you agree with the southern Africa bishops' claim that condoms are an inappropriate solution, what steps do you think would more successfully stem the AIDS epidemic? Please explain your answers.

3. John C. Caldwell argues that African governments need to become more involved in the fight against AIDS, while Alison Katz asserts that the Western response to the African AIDS cri-

sis is racist and imperialist. After reading their viewpoints, who do you think would have more success reducing AIDS in Africa, African governments or international organizations? Explain your answer.

Chapter 3

1. After reading the articles in this chapter, which policy do you believe will have the most positive impact on Africa? Are there other policies, not suggested by the authors, that you think would be more effective? Explain your answers.

2. If free trade can bring peace between African nations and end political corruption, as Thompson Ayodele asserts, would that offset the troubling economic effects posited by Leon P. Spencer? Can the success of free trade only be measured monetarily or can it have a political aspect? Explain your answers.

3. Florence Wambugu, an African scientist and employee of Monsanto, argues that Europeans should not tell Africans to reject genetically modified food, because Europeans do not understand the reality of hunger and poverty. Do you think she makes her argument from the perspective of an African or as an employee of a company known for developing GM crops? Explain your answer.

Chapter 4

1. After reading the viewpoints in this chapter, which of the policies discussed, if any, do you think will be most effective at preserving Africa's environment? What other policies would you suggest? Explain your answers.

2. Michael De Alessi and the Humane Society of the United States disagree on the effects that trade in ivory could have on Africa's elephant population. Whose argument do you think better addresses the concerns of Africans and why?

3. One of the arguments made repeatedly in this chapter is that Africans will be more willing to guard their wild lands if they can benefit economically by doing so. Do you believe that Africans need a monetary incentive to preserve their environment or do you feel that such a conclusion too readily assumes that a capitalist approach will be welcome in non-Western nations? Explain your answers.

Organizations to Contact

The editors have compiled the following list of organizations concerned with the issues debated in this book. The descriptions are derived from materials provided by the organizations. All have publications or information available for interested readers. The list was compiled on the date of publication of the present volume; the information provided here may change. Be aware that many organizations take several weeks or longer to respond to inquiries, so allow as much time as possible.

Africa Action
1634 Eye St. NW, #810, Washington, DC 20006
(202) 546-7961 • fax: (202) 546-1545
e-mail: africaaction@igc.org • website: www.africapolicy.org
Africa Action is a national organization that uses analysis and public pressure to change U.S. and international policy toward Africa, in the hopes of achieving political, social, and economic justice. The website offers an e-journal with policy documents dating back to 1995, as well as information on debt, health care, and other resources on issues relating to Africa.

Africare
440 R St. NW, Washington, DC 20001
(202) 462-3614 • fax: (202) 387-1034
e-mail: development@africare.org • website: www.africare.org
Africare is one of America's leading private charitable organizations assisting Africa. Its programs emphasize issues such as agriculture, health, education, and the environment. The organization has offices throughout Africa that aid in the development of the continent. Africare issues annual reports, and a newsletter, editorials, and speeches are also available on its website.

Canada Fund for Africa (CFA)
Canadian International Development Agency
200 Promenade de Portage, Hull, Quebec, K1A 0G4 Canada
(819) 934-1156 • fax: (819) 953-5845
e-mail: canadafundafrica@acdi-cida.gc.ca
website: www.cida.gc.ca/canadafundforafrica
The CFA, which is part of the Canadian International Development Agency, works closely with African governments and organizations in order to help African nations cope with issues such as HIV/AIDS and peace and security. In addition CFA supports in-

creased investment in Africa as a way to encourage economic growth and to help reduce poverty.

Foundation for Democracy in Africa
1900 L St. NW, Suite 414, Washington, DC 20036
(202) 331-1333 • fax: (202) 331-8547
e-mail: comments@democracy-africa.org
website: http://democracy-africa.org

The Foundation for Democracy in Africa is a nonpartisan organization whose mission is to bring democratic government and economic opportunity to Africa. The foundation provides education, training, and technical support to African leaders in order to achieve these aims. The foundation also conducts research and holds seminars on issues facing Africa.

International Monetary Fund
700 19th St. NW, Washington, DC 20431
(202) 623-7300 • fax: (202) 623-6278
e-mail: publicaffairs@imf.org • website: www.imf.org

The IMF is an international organization of 184 countries that promotes international monetary cooperation and stable exchange arrangements in order to encourage global economic growth. The fund also provides temporary financial assistance to countries to help ease debt payments. The organization issues an annual report and fact sheets.

Oxfam International
Suite 20, 266 Banbury Rd., Oxford, OX2 7DL UK
++ 44 1865 31 39 39 / 36 39 • fax: ++ 44 1865 31 37 70
e-mail: information@oxfaminternational.org
website: www.oxfaminternational.org

Oxfam International is a confederation of twelve organizations that work together to develop solutions to poverty and injustice. Its members, who live in more than one hundred countries, use popular campaigns and communications work to help lobby for policies that will most effectively address the issues surrounding global poverty. A variety of publications can be found on Oxfam's website, including annual reports, speeches, and policy papers.

United Nations Development Programme (UNDP)
One United Nations Plaza, New York, NY 10017
fax: (212) 906-5364
e-mail: enquiries@undp.org • website: www.undp.org

The goals of the UNDP include helping developing nations reduce poverty, establish democratic governments, improve the quality of their environments, and reduce the transmission of HIV/AIDS. UNDP publications include the annual *Human Development Report* and the quarterly magazine *Choices.*

U.S. State Department Bureau of African Affairs
U.S. Department of State
2201 C St. NW, Washington, DC 20520
(202) 647-4000
e-mail: secretary@state.gov • website: www.state.gov/p/af
The Bureau of African Affairs guides the operation of U.S. diplomats in sub-Saharan Africa and advises the Secretary of State. The bureau provides fact sheets, reports, briefings, and background information on Africa.

World Bank
1818 H St. NW, Washington, DC 20433
(202) 473-1000 • fax: (202) 477-6391
website: www.worldbank.org
The World Bank, a specialized agency of the United Nations, is one of the world's largest sources of development assistance. The 184 member nations of the World Bank work jointly to determine which efforts the organization should help fund, typically in fields such as health care, education, and the environment. In 2003 the World Bank provided $18.5 billion and worked in more than one hundred developing nations. The organization publishes a *World Development Report* each year, along with other reports and books.

Website

AllAfrica
website: www.AllAfrica.com
AllAfrica.com is a multimedia website that posts more than eight hundred stories on Africa each day. The website, which has four offices worldwide, also features a searchable archive containing more than six hundred thousand articles.

Bibliography of Books

Guy Arnold — *A Guide to African Political and Economic Development.* London: Fitzroy Dearborn, 2001.

George B.N. Ayittey — *Africa Unchained: The Blueprint for Africa's Future.* Basingstoke, England: Palgrave Macmillan, 2004.

Bill Berkeley — *The Graves Are Not Yet Full: Race, Tribe, and Power in the Heart of Africa.* New York: Basic Books, 2001.

Frederick Cooper — *Africa Since 1940: The Past of the Present.* New York: Cambridge University Press, 2002.

Michael Darkoh and Apollo Rwomire, eds. — *Human Impact on Environment and Sustainable Development in Africa.* Aldershot, England: Ashgate, 2003.

Jillian Edelstein — *Truth and Lies: Stories from the Truth and Reconciliation Commission in South Africa.* New York: New Press, 2002.

Lyn S. Graybill — *Truth and Reconciliation in South Africa: Miracle or Model?* Boulder, CO: Lynne Rienner, 2002.

Emma Guest — *Children of AIDS: Africa's Orphan Crisis.* London: Pluto Press, 2001.

Robert Harvey — *The Fall of Apartheid: The Inside Story from Smuts to Mbeki.* New York: Palgrave, 2001.

Ankie Hoogvelt — *Globalization and the Postcolonial World: The New Political Economy of Development.* Baltimore: Johns Hopkins University Press, 2001.

Mark Huband — *The Skull Beneath the Skin: Africa After the Cold War.* Boulder, CO: Westview Press, 2001.

Susan Hunter — *Black Death: AIDS in Africa.* Basingstoke, England: Palgrave Macmillan, 2003.

Goran Hyden, Hastings W.O. Okoth-Ogendo, and Bamidele Olowu, eds. — *African Perspectives on Governance.* Trenton, NJ: Africa World Press, 2000.

Robert D. Kaplan — *Surrender or Starve: Travels in Sudan, Ethiopia, Somalia, and Eritrea.* London: Vintage Books, 2003.

Carol Lancaster — *Aid to Africa: So Much to Do, So Little Done.* Chicago: University of Chicago Press, 1999.

Ricardo René Laremont, ed. — *The Causes of War and the Consequences of Peacekeeping in Africa.* Portsmouth, NH: Heinemann, 2002.

Richard E. Mshomba · *Africa in the Global Economy.* Boulder, CO: Lynne Rienner, 2000.

Godfrey Mwakikagile · *Economic Development in Africa.* Commack, NY: Nova Science, 1999.

Andrew Norman · *Robert Mugabe and the Betrayal of Zimbabwe.* Jefferson, NC: McFarland, 2003.

John-Peter Pham · *Liberia: Portrait of a Failed State.* New York: Reed Press, 2004.

Alan Rake · *African Leaders: Guiding the New Millennium.* Lanham, MD: Scarecrow Press, 2001.

M.A. Mohamed Salih · *African Democracies and African Politics.* London: Pluto Press, 2001.

Richard Sandbrook · *Closing the Circle: Democratization and Development in Africa.* New York: Zed Books, 2000.

Ronald Segal · *Islam's Black Slaves: The Other Black Diaspora.* New York: Farrar, Straus and Giroux, 2001.

Joseph James Shomon · *Wild Edens: Africa's Premier Game Parks and Their Wildlife.* College Station: Texas A&M University Press, 1998.

Allister Sparks · *Beyond the Miracle: Inside the New South Africa.* Chicago: University of Chicago Press, 2003.

Leonard Thompson · *A History of South Africa.* New Haven, CT: Yale University Press, 2001.

Yvonne M. Tsikata · *Globalisation, Poverty and Inequality in Sub-Saharan Africa: A Political Economy Appraisal.* Paris: OECD Development Centre, 2001.

Desmond Mpilo Tutu · *No Future Without Forgiveness.* New York: Doubleday, 2000.

Joachim Von Braun et al. · *Famine in Africa: Causes, Responses, and Prevention.* Baltimore: Johns Hopkins University Press, 2000.

Gabriel I.H. Williams · *Liberia: The Heart of Darkness.* Victoria, Canada: Trafford, 2002.

Donald Woods · *Rainbow Nation Revisited: South Africa's Decade of Democracy.* London: Andre Deutsch, 2004.

Index

UNAIDS (United Nations Program on AIDS), 90
United States
  anti-AIDS drugs access and, 60–62
  arrogance of, 136
  ban on ivory imports to, 160
  position on GM foods, 149–51
  role of, in Liberia, 110–11
urbanization, 15

viremia, 96

Wambugu, Florence, 138–44
Weissman, Robert, 58
Western, David, 184
Whitehouse, David, 15
whites
  attacks against, in Zimbabwe, 43
  oppress blacks in South Africa, 46–53
  prejudice against, in South Africa, 41–45
Wijnstekers, Willem, 160
wilderness
  African traditions and preservation of, 190–94
  local control will protect, 180–85
  tourism can help protect, 165–72
  con, 173–79
  see also conservation
wildlife preservation
  African traditions and, 190–92

controlling hunting will help, 186–89
  vs. humans, 181–82
  ivory trade will help, 156–60
  con, 161–64
  local control is best for, 180–85
  tourism can help, 165–72
  see also endangered species
women
  AIDS in, 56–57
  vulnerability of, 94, 95
World Food Program (WFP), 146
World Society for the Protection of Animals (WSPA), 157–58
World Trade Organization (WTO), 60–61

Zaire, 19
Zambia, 149–50
Ziegler, Jean, 151
Zimbabwe
  agricultural problems in, 15
  AIDS in, 90
  attacks against whites in, 43
  conservation efforts in, 154
  economic problems in, 29
  elephant population in, 158
  famine in, 147
  politics in, 36
Zoellick, Robert B., 131
Zulus, 193–94